AF661005

AMERICAN INTERVENTIONS AND JUST CAUSE

The Rationale behind the Oregon Trail

Dr. Manan Dwivedi

Foreword by

Yogendra Narain
Former Secretary General of Rajya Sabha and
India's Former Defense Secretary

PENTAGON PRESS LLP

American Interventions and Just Cause: The Rationale behind the Oregon Trail
by Dr. Manan Dwivedi

ISBN 978-93-86618-88-7

First Published in 2019

Copyright © Dr. Manan Dwivedi

All rights reserved. No part of this publication may be reproduced, stored in a retrieval system, or transmitted in any form or by any means, electronic, mechanical, photocopying, recording or otherwise, without the prior written permission of the Publisher.

Disclaimer: The views and opinions expressed in the book are the individual assertion of the Author. The Publisher does not take any responsibility for the same in any manner whatsoever. The same shall solely be the responsibility of the Author.

Published by
PENTAGON PRESS LLP
206, Peacock Lane, Shahpur Jat,
New Delhi-110049
Phones: 011-64706243, 26491568
Telefax: 011-26490600
email: rajan@pentagonpress.in
website: www.pentagonpress.in

Contents

FOREWORD

IN his book, the author Manan, has covered the entire gamut of interventions, by the United States of America in countries not only near the mainland but also the Far East, Middle East , Afghanistan as well as South Asia. Because of its economic clout as well as military might the USA has acted as the policeman of the world and intervenes wherever and whenever it feels that its interests are getting adversely affected. Notwithstanding the tenets of international law it has sent its forces on the slightest pretext as was the case in IRAQ. The existence of weapons of mass destruction is still not proved. USA ignores the United Nation organisation and acts on its own ignoring the very principles of respect of sovereignty of nations which is the cornerstone of the edifice of the UNO.

The present policies of the United States in walking out of treaties like in Iran has caused misgivings not only in the Middle East but also in Europe. The sudden decision to walk out of Afghanistan on the plea of bringing the forces back home and at the same time continuing to intervene in Syria shows unpredictability. USA must realise that it is no longer a unipolar world. The author has rightly pointed out that USA cannot ignore another reality i.e. the growth of China both as an economic and military power. Russia is already unhappy with USA because of the sanctions imposed on it. Attempts to control the development of nuclear weapons by North Korea have not succeeded.

The internal conflict between the US Congress and the President is having its effect both internally and externally. With the President demanding an increase in military spending and more money for construction of a border wall, there will be sharp cuts to domestic programmes like education and environment as well as to the mandatory safety net programmes like Medicaid. The author has very correctly pointed out that domestic unrest will lead to uncertainty in the US policy abroad. The author has clinically analysed the leadership of the USA in fighting the ISIS as well as terrorism all over the world. On one side in Syria USA. is using its military proweress but in Afghanistan it is negotiating with the Taliban. Countries like India depend on the USA for controlling terrorist attacks from Pakistan but on the other hand USA wants Pakistan help in talks with the Taliban. China is an all weather friend of Pakistan and in a turn of events Pakistan is no longer getting recognition as an ally of USA. The USA now supports India vis-a-vis Pakistan in the Security Council but in the Trade war threatens to remove all the duty benefits given to India, as India has not reduced the tariff on the Harley motor bikes

The author has highlighted how the whims of the US President have affected American policy. It has been a long road from isolationism in the past to the interventionist policy of USA today. Power brings responsibility and the rest of the countries in the world would like the USA to be a leader not only economically and militarily but in protection of the environment as well as in the elimination of poverty. The future will show whether these expectations would be realised.

Yogendra Narain
Former Secretary General of Rajya Sabha and
India's Former Defense Secretary

Prologue et al

PRESIDENT Trump declared in his stately State of the Union Address, 2019, 'To rebuild and revitalize our nation's infrastructure, to reduce the price of health care and prescription drugs, to create an immigration system that is safe, lawful, modern, and secure and to pursue a foreign policy that puts America's interests first. There is a new opportunity in American politics if only we have the courage together to seize it'.

The American victory is not a Republican victory but is the nation's general and comprehensive progression. What to expect, when the entire rant of the Global and sections of Domestic Media circulates a diatribe against the founding fathers and the fundamental tenets of US Foreign Policy and its multifarious interventions across the larger international system wherein the Asiatic/Oriental solidarity is a term that is much bandied about for ideological and thematic perspectives and positioning. The larger legerdemain of President Trump is being targeted by some sections of the Global academia and Media that does not amount to a sustained striving by the larger Fourth Estate.

President Trump since being the Presumptive American President has taken a multitude of path-breaking decisions including the rousing call to construct the non-malleable Mexican wall, Immigration reforms along with indicating a gradual withdrawal of the American Overarch from its crucial West Asian Responsibilities. Lest he forget the dictum that 'With Great Power Comes Great Responsibility'. The stress of the Book and the avowed objective is to perceive the larger rubric of the American Interventions all across the conflict hot spots through a convergent fork of Ideology and Real Politic better defined as national interest in the true blue philanthropic resolve of the United States of America. The Primal fear and the objective of the work is to mount a spirited but subtle defence of the American wars and interventions in the twilight-zone nations of the World Polity through references and multiple evidence from ICJ case law and UN Charter legalese that can metamorphose the United States to being a Regulator and Peacenik Leader of the Democratic and the liberal international order with the NSS rendering by President Trump in 2017 in order to coax New Delhi and Prime Minister Narendra Modi as the Vishwaguru in the larger global polity where potential leads to performativity. The work zeroes in on the larger philanthropy of United States in regions with contested sovereignties. The Book strives to be a panegyric for American strength, verve and power with the avowed vocation for letting the man in steel alight on the crown of Statue of Liberty with his love interest, Lana Lang in the twinkling stars all around the skyscape.

Acknowledgment

FINALLY, a well meaning "thankfulness epistle" has to be drafted! What Bliss!!! In this Mt. Sinai oriented academic and innovation experiment of mine, loyalty towards the American schemata and its larger relevance for bringing in peace and solidity for the international system in its conflict hot spots has set me on to this benighted endeavor that might be construed as a cudgel to beat the anarchists with.

This labor of love and work of academe art, would not have reached a fruition without the blessings of my mother, whom every folk calls as the grand Dadi to my daughter, Pal Dwivedi, a toddler she adores very much. She has a quaint silent walk at midnights when she is the sole provider of coffee, black tea and popcorn to me as I read on or type away at my homestead word processor. It is this benevolent vocation that steered me through with respectable ease since my first tête-à-tête with the CBSE Boards. She has always kept alive the verve of humble honesty, steady steadfastness of character and wellbeing along with a wherewithal to evade stately nepotism and graft that and the ant-nepotic sentiment which ran in my Pa's veins and has been kept alive by the indomitable spirit of our loving and caring, "Dadi". She inspires me on to write and read and read and write again, as an inescapable chore that ties me with my soul and entire wellbeing. Akin to my Pa, America has been a longing for her, too. Her Saturday shopping sprees of Utensils for the hearth keep me engaged and in return she boils black tea for me. Some Motherly vocation!!!!!!!!! Some contend that we have not seen God, which is rather untrue as the mother figure is God incarnate for us!!!!!!!

Pojs Dwivedi, my better half, has inspired me to work on relentlessly despite the excesses of Stately obfuscations, and her inspired striving to take up all the household legerdemain has left me with enough evening time to conjure my argument in soft. Pal Dwivedi, my daughter, has been indefatigably against my sittings expecting me to tend to her doll houses and soft toys and pitch in the fun tenet for her in the drawing room. My rationale to her that Pa needs to read and write in order to earn bread and get her toys is finally an argument that satiates her tiny self and she lets me off from her toys and doughty home assignments. Some kindergarten task as she too gets the patriotic tenet after watching Uri and Manikarnika with me!!!!!!!!

Prof. Sushma Yadav, and now VC at a renowned University has been a relentless source of unbridled inspiration in this academic endeavor of mine, wherein she worked with me on projects and seminar proposals at IIPA. The astuteness of her academic precision was gleaned by me rather selfishly to my tangible gains. Dr. Hemant Khare, the Assistant Librarian, facilitated me with the research material to a great extent with his awesome simplicity and great intellect, true to his schooling at Pandit Deen Dayal Upadhyaya Vidyalaya in Kanpur. My maternal uncles too need more than a mention as they facilitated my civility in toto after my Pa left for his heavenly abode in 2011. My *nana*, Prof. Gopinath Sharma, is another personage who dedicated his entire life in chiseling the Mewar's narrative in medieval history, and his incessant attempts to make me do correct pronunciations, preferably the British, leave me remembering my Daisha, even today. His doughty rendering of the visage of Maharana Pratap Singh, the ruler of Mewar, lingers on in the contemporary history as Maharana Ratan Singh contends to Rani Padmini standing aloft the ramparts of the Chittorgarh fort, "Rani Sa Samay Agaya hai", which means that the time has come to battle the psychic and psychedelic Khalji as fire balls start disfiguring the sanguine beauty of the historic Chittorgarh fort.

Prof. Chintamani Mahapatra with his unstinting performativity as an academic par excellence has been a persistent source of inspiration and performance. Sir is a performance artist with his immense and hallowed expertise in the sphere of the American stream of study. Sir's alacrity in accepting my invitations to him for my APPPA IR course has made me develop a second innings connect with his benign and preponderant self. His larger-than-life academic visage underlines what all I have written till date on America. His choice of Prof. Ventaramani's papers which were taught to my batch, has left an insatiable urge to read all his anointed work. Hopefully, I can be the "bot", in the Hollywood Flick Short Circuit, in this salient context.

Prof. Ashwini Mahapatra at JNU has re-invented in me the urge to go the Indic way in IR theorizing and his unstinting strivings in bringing sanity and mainstream thought processes in JNU. This tenet has brought me closer to his benign self as his nonchalant ease at lectures initiates me on a new odyssey at Teen Murthi Library. Sunil Ambekarji has been akin to a beacon with his unstinting Karyakarta work along with his gargantuan intellect as inspiring other Karyakartas.

Yogendra Narain sir, Former Chief Secretary, UP, and India's former Defense Secretary, has an indefatigable charm and his attendant panache has been a great motif for me at IIPA, who calls me his, "Find". His immensely experienced and royal approach towards encouraging younglings like me, has, left an inedible impression upon my personage. It's all due to U Sir!!!

Dr. Rajeev Nayan and Dr. Uttam Sinha, from the Institute of Defense Studies and Analysis, have been the soul's wit behind my recent work as their unstinting suggestions helped me traverse the criterion of writing in a much organized manner. They have been the Force Majore to make me re invent my super powers and fly away to academic glory and recognition. Especially, "Leadership for the cause" enlightened me to my new national service roles as my second tryst with destiny. Prof. Harsh Pant at King's College gave me an opportunity to follow the idiom of brevity and encouraged me on to better academic work that includes giving a positive review for book *Serendipity and the American Dream*. Mritunjay Tripathi, my good friend from the Global Jindal School, has contributed a chapter in this labor of love as he initiates a noavae and fresh career for himself in academia. Here's to the unstinting spirit of Youth!!!

DR. MANAN DWIVEDI

“For Gatiya Pa”

"Papadamoak" ... in the Oregon Trail

THE nomenclature of Papadamoak stands for my diminutively doughty but fighter Pa who passed away in the fateful rains of 2011. Pa has nothing to do with the Bollywood saga of Pa starring as Amitabh Bachchan my Pa was my very own Gatiya Pa and Vinod Khanna par excellence. Pa is known even now amongst family elders as the *Mumbai ka protagonist* who declared grossly in Dungarpur that no one else but he would tie nuptials with my Ma and now our Dadi. Pa had a well-delineated streak for combating nepotism at his work place in Jaipur, which made him a kind of Vigilante.

Pa began his life's odyssey with his quintessential Vicky that could carry four personages with dexterous and efficient ease. He graduated on to a Priya scooter that paved the way for my scintillating Kinetic Honda and then my wedding car bearing the graffiti, "Dear Supes" at the back mirror! Pa's last World Cup cricket tryst drove the lives out of Team India's adversaries and we both drove out of Gandhinagar in Gujarat to have sweet betel at twelve in the night. Pa used to relate that his sole dream scenario of driving around India Gate has been realized in a timely manner but he needed to redeem his pledge with Destiny by driving around the Capital Hill, which I had promised but this Dream evaporated as he separated ways with the ways of the world. It is here that my American vocation was initiated that had been strengthened by my *Nai Sarak* American Comics, novellas and books on American History and what all Books I won at the Shankar's Art Competition and at Galgotia's, CP, as a child artist.

Pa instilled the professional veneer in my uncivilized soul by cannily referring to the American civilization, the nation, its people, and most important of all, the American congruence with Indian ethics in the political firmament, shared values, was what he religiously hankered after!!!!! He hated the Domed Ruskies and had fallen for the DC character of Kal El aka Superman and the genre of American superiority in what all existed in the comity of nations; he wanted India to emulate the American experiment without the "shoddy and unkempt edges of buildings and cars in Moscow". All in all, America for me is as good as what my Pa thought and ruminated about it as his tongue would often dislodge the twin artificial canines in his mouth!!!! And that's how the character of Count Dracula took a re-birth in our household and family lore. But, akin to Uncle Ben in the Movie Spiderman, he never stressed on responsibility for me thus turning me into a luftmensch that I grew up to be later on!!!! The lotus-eating sinews got exposed as the exigencies of the system dawned on to me and the only theme of his times, which I negate now, is his unstinting belief in the veracity of the system holders being welfarist city Czars. But, still, he always was proud of the fact that his own unsure, sullen and bespectacled boy never filled up the UPSC form and intentionally and not incidentally, chose his own dear vocation in the academia. He was a believer which I was too, till he left us high and dry. It is these schisms, vagaries of mutual congruence and Pa's versatile traits that enamor me to my American Dream converging on to my father's layman framework of a civilizational tryst between New Delhi and Washington. My PM Modi has fortunately realized that for us as his New India's ally-hood with United States of America.

1

A Stealthy Backgrounder to Tangible, Intangible and Imagined Conceptualizations of American Interventions

MY Lai, Green Zone, the Noriega Palace, taverns of the tantalising Tora Bora and the mystery MOAB! All these arcane sounding words have a common string linking them. That linkage happens to be that of American interventions. The United States of America is a nation par excellence with overgrown and pending global role-playing responsibilities and popular expectations for yeomanly acts that firm up a difficult-to-live-up-to philanthropic resolve. The nation reverberates with the bluster and verve of being a quintessential and stereotypical Regulator nation in the larger international system. Despite the inward-looking parlance of homeland security, as advanced by President Donald Trump, once the presumptive Republican Candidate in the electoral jamboree of 2016, the nation atop Mount Sinai has perennially strived to intervene in conflict scenarios amidst the rigmarole of failed and failing nations. This makes the go gooder hyper State, stand tall with its objective of the Global Demos. We need to ruminate and chew over the debates of the order of: Why does United States of America need to democratize the larger neighbourhood? And, what legal, democratic and political legerdermian it needs to adhere to, so, as to escape the malevolent appellation of being a crudely interventionist nation state?

The onus lies with the audience, chosen state heads such as PM Narendra Modi, President Putin, Premier Xi Xingpin, and the decision-makers of the

World Polity in order to circumvent the staid argument of 'American illegality' and 'American Illegitimacy', where-in, the nation with a Manifest Destiny has regularly intervened in national principalities such as Philippines, world wars, Europe, Serbia, Kosovo, the Korean Peninsula, Vietnam, the larger Indo-China, Dominican Republic, Nicaragua, Iraq, Syria, Libya and other conflict prone and unguided states. The need for an American economic pelf and security is a notion that exists in the contemporary and the turbulent context of the larger international system, where-in, US emerges as the nation of the last resort. International organizations such as United Nations and EU, and other regional conglomerates of global cooperation have been found wanting in the realm of fire-fighting hotchpotches in alien but besieged nations and societies. The grandiloquent American penchant for philanthropy and the Don-Juan invocation in its foreign policy sometimes stands alone as a much ravaged policy instrumentality. Still, the intentions have been an avid amalgamation of the fulfilment of national interest imbued with a messianic zeal of restoring order in 'torn states and societies'.

The 'Protest Start' of the Trump and the American Regime: January 2017 Revisited

The American turbulence with the coming to the stead of President Trump and the attendant and burgeoning turbulence caused by the anointment, will have to be read and astutely comprehended as a first—Up objective. It is amidst these VIBGYOR and mutating times, in the nation's political firmament, that, the American notion of the grand overarch through its station-oriented moral crusades, can be conveniently analysed. This search for a context brings us home to the 'Trump times', in Washington and the larger world.

President Trump will be known for his bravado and bluster come what may as subtleties elude him. President Trump has emerged, not only as an American phenomenon but also as a global phenomenon that militates against the traditional and conventional comprehension of governance and foreign policy decision making in the larger sense of the term. President Trump faces an uphill task in the aftermath of the convergence of women interests and an American Federal Court's ruling against his executive order to curtail the entry of denizens from states such as Libya, Syria, Iraq, Iran, Somalia and a few other rogue and failed nations. These drastic methods are living true to his campaign trail promises of sequestering a few national populations from the land of milk and honey that have ushered in a mass level of protests and vituperations, by, prominent interests and sections of populations in the United States. They threaten to attach a pariah status to the new President as if the Democrat lobbies along with the Clinton establishment were not enough obfuscations to the governance trail of President Trump.

According to a headline in the British daily, *The Independent*, the headline declares that women hate Trump so much that they are marching against him not only around Capitol Hill but also in the ravages of an austere Antarctica. Moves are also on to bring back Barrack Obama to the forefront as a returning President that is definitely unconstitutional. This seemingly appears to be a politically phantasmagorical approach. Though the polls during the campaign trail declared earlier on that single women with children were supporting candidate Hillary Clinton, still the outcome of the US Presidential Elections pinpointed otherwise, as, the nation elected Donald Trump over the politically correct and a pro-establishment, Hillary Clinton. It is this novae trail of the alternate way of doing politics, governance, elections and foreign policy that has become the cornerstone of the American Dream, which President Trump intends to objectify as the new Oregon trail of our very own American nation and an Indian ally, as declared by the US National Security Strategy which also posits a strategically crucial, "Leader and Regulator Role Play" for the Vishwaguru oriented Indian nation. Thus, the Trump's Dream ushers the coming of the new Diva, that is the Indic Vishwaguru in a Realist sense of the term driven by the dexterous and effervescently likeable Regime of Prime Minister Narendra Modi.

Also, as an attendant fact, both the sides of the coin need to be perceived clearly if a true reading of the political tumult in United States has to be reached that was actually tumultuous. It has been globally reported that thousands of women 'marched on' on the day of the Presidential inauguration in over 60 countries with the larger objective to protest in the favour of, 'Women Rights, Human Rights and against hate'.[1] As an extraordinary instance of protest, 30 women have marched in the Paradise Bay located in Antarctica that is populated by Wendell Seals, Hunchback whales and Gentoo penguins. They raised slogans such as, 'Penguins for Peace, Seals for Science, Cormorants for Climate and Love from Seven Continents'.[2]

What might be the consequence of these initial moves and bills that have been tabled by the Republican Government? In the economic sphere, Donald

Trump went against the Trans-Pacific Partnership (TPP) that was originally meant to counter the Regional Comprehensive Economic Partnership (RCEP) agreement considered to be a grouping of nations meant to serve the interests of a pro-Beijing lobby and the diplomatic denomination. This is one reading of the situation. The TPP led by Washington could have worked as a counterweight to RCEP but that does not stand any more as a proposal and now by the end of 2018, RCEP is making rigorous progression in the Asian realm. The American withdrawal places stress on nations such as India, in, the larger Asiatic Space where-in, the nations that are being encircled by China will be facing a regional power vacuum in the absence of United States as it intends to leave behind allies in South East Asia and new strategic partners such as India. Also, President Trump has projected himself as a personage who has rebelled against "the politically correct graft" that had been institutionalized in the United States of America by the Democrats.

Immigration curbs have become the centre of the storm, with the Trump declaration on the refugee policy too coming up for global criticism. The curb on the H-IB visas comprise the entry of one of the largest number of Indians from 2013 onwards that led to the trying development that the Indian software giants might face difficulties in the future. As an attendant fact, Google and FB groups along with other corporate groups can find a way out of the executive order passed by the Trump administration. With Indians being employed in the firm, Microsoft, the firm has applied with the American establishment to let in some of its 'responsible and sincere workers' despite recently introduced immigration curbs. President Trump's executive order also includes some exemptions for the companies to request and create a legitimate way out for looking out for case-specific treatment while bringing workforce from other countries. Indian firms have to take the route followed by Microsoft, as, they too are set to lose a King's pie, by, the January executive order that places curbs on the H-1B and L-1 visas that are primarily work visas and non-immigrant ones, over, the top of that. This abrupt H-1B visa curb policy reflects homeland security–related protectionism that does not present an easy picture for the Software firms in India trading with the market in the United States. Still, President Trump ideally prognosticated that he will strategically mellow down his standpoint on immigration, which he has done promptly and astutely with the idiom of advocating 'meritocracy' as the backbone of the American immigration thought and policy.[3] It's similar to the skillocracy of PM Narendra Modi in New Delhi.

Coming back to the trap of the sea of protests against President Trump, it is rather surprising that the same people who voted for President Trump are rallying around a reason for opposing the elected American President. Apart from the individual issues, which have been opposed by the domestic protesters in the United States, the question that deserves a learned answer is, 'Why is the new, "America-First Approach" invented and propagated by President Trump, is being opposed so largely and stringently by a large section of the people in the United States of America'? The thinning out of the Trump wave might be one probable answer but that seems highly improbable as a larger popular and political game-plan by the opposition interests might be the force behind the sea of protests being registered against the Trump administration. Marisa Franco, as reported in the *New Yorker*, was the brain behind organizing the initial protests against President Trump. She is reported to have said, 'Inauguration Day marks the beginning of the nightmare for millions of people across the country. For many of us, we simply cannot afford to hold onto a hollow hope that Trump will change course on the disasters he pledged in his campaign. We understand that we have to use everything in our power to resist and force a detour from taking us all backwards'.[4]

The coming times will test the veracity of the claims and the counter-claims as even Iran, which was promised a sanctions-free life, has declared that the 'Evil State's' wrestlers will not be allowed entry to participate in a global wrestling competition to be organized in Iran. The future of the Iran–US and the West-brokered nuclear deal also rests in uncertainty with the Iranian act of testing a ballistic missile being read by the American administration as an act of abrogating the nuclear deal with the West and the United Nations that was brokered by the former President Barrack Obama. In 2018, President Trump has moved out of the Nuclear deal which drastically changes the power equation in the region. The protests that have been a kind of gathering storm in various places in the United States, have precedents too. Though not on such a large scale, but, such gatherings were organized as a prelude to the Presidential years of President Nixon and President George Bush. The larger question is, 'Can the sea of protests strengthened by the Federal Court be read as a backlash against the conservative skill set of the present American administration'? We intend to open a can of worms with positing such an above-written narrative of the American homeland turf. *The question that this tome will seek to ponder upon in the rest of the content narrative is, 'How can the United States and its larger-than-life-symbolic Statue of Liberty, the mascot of Mt Rushmore and the shining walk of fame in Hollywood, with a turbulent political tide, stand forth in isolation? Will the America as we know, it withdraw in its own uncharacteristic shell and shy away from global crusades worth its salt? Or how can we posit the umpteen American military interventions and moral crusades across the decades in the context of "those" times and the present avid interjections in the year 2017 and beyond'? Thus, the outward, inclusive and zealous overarch of the American nation is the fundamental myth and lore with its quintessential legalities and the much castigated illegalities, which will be borne as the staple subject content in the novae narrative that will clinically unfold before the discerning readership.*

Finally, America under Trump refuses to be a non-interventionist state and it never be a non-interventionist state with its avowedly Global responsibilities.

The Schism and President Donald Trump: America and Saudi Arabia Up Close and Personal

President Trump tweeted from his Twitter account on landing in Saudi Arabia, on 20 May 2017, where-in the Saudi state head was brought in an aircraft car to receive President Trump. The tweet expressed, 'I have reached Riyadh and I am looking forward to the afternoon and the evening that lies ahead'. The royal welcome accorded to President Trump happens to be that of a phalanx of red, white and blue contrails, as the Air Force One hovered over Riyadh and the terminology used by the Saudi leaders has been that of being 'Historic'. The multi-story image of the President was another mainstay of the larger paraphernalia that accompanies President Trump's visit to Saudi Arabia. The entire rubric of the crusade against Islamic State and fundamentalist terror happens to be a prime-time concern of the American dream and the intent to prepare the homeland and protect it with repeated fusillades against the global spread of the terror group *internationale.*

The entire visit and the strivings of the American Empire are pitted against the rising overarch of Islamic terror that has already expressed its slithering expanse and impactful malfeasance in the nations premised in the European continent apart from the "territorial avatar" of ISIS in the hotly contested terrain of West Asia. Since a few years, the United States has been attempting to forge a consensual coalition, as, an adjunct to the Global, 'War on Terror', which envisages the "Sunni NATO" nations such as Saudi Arabia that can go ahead with the annihilation of the Shia expanse in West Asia. Also, the United States made attempts to normalize bilateral relations with Iran but with the advent of President Trump, that thought pattern in the policy reaches a change. Washington's strivings are advancing on to forge a bond with the NATO countries with twilight-zone nations, such as Turkey and the traditional allies such as Saudi Arabia. The efforts have always been on the anvil in order to cobble together an edifice and a coalition, to counter the Shia group of nations. Thus, an international front to counter Global Jihadi terror can be what the 'Global-Peace-Doctor' ordered for the day.

The controversial earnestness with which President has donned the mantle in the United States is part of the Global strivings with the objective being the containment of global terror groups such as ISIS, Boko Haram, Al Qaeda, etc. The allegation that can be labelled at Washington is that the strike potential that has been unleashed over West Asia has not been replicated with the Korean antagonist who is a perennial nation state actor that is recalcitrant in its ways and posturing. Still, the June, 2018 Daredevil Summitry with Pyongyong has enabled the larger world system not to walk over the precipice of war with North Korea agreeing to a western framework of disarmament and regional peace. The Committee on Foreign Relations too informs,

> Islam's schism, simmering for fourteen centuries, doesn't explain all the political, economic, and geostrategic factors involved in these conflicts, but it has become one prism through which to understand the underlying tensions. Two countries that compete for the leadership of Islam, Sunni Saudi Arabia and Shia Iran, have used the sectarian divide to further their ambitions. How their rivalry is settled will likely shape the political balance between Sunnis and Shias and the future of the region, especially in Syria, Iraq, Lebanon, Bahrain, and Yemen.[5]

There is a proxy battle that has always been fought with the Jihadi terror mongers attempting a novae façade of unity to wage a war of attrition against Islamic Terror. Historically, too, the succession matter over who had to be anointed as the head of the religion, was formed that divided Islam into twin sects of Shias and Sunnis. It was Ali Ibn Abi Talib, who formed the name around which the Shias collaborated and congealed as one part of the Islamic Schism. The Sunnis remained as the followers of the group of Mohammad. It is this sectarian divide that has been the brimstone over which several West

Asian conflicts have been spawned, and the myriad nations from outside the religion and the region have been involved in the regional drama as it unfolded through the last few decades in the twilight zone of international polity. The treatment meted out to the non-Arab moslems too became a schism in the region and the Arab and non-Arab regions, on the whole. Down in South Asia, PM Narendra Modi has finally destroyed terror camps in PoK and signalled the Indian protest against state terror in February, 2018.

An American web portal informs us, 'Iran's Islamic Revolution in 1979 gave Shia cleric, Ayatollah Ruhollah Khomeini, the opportunity to implement his vision for an Islamic government ruled by the "guardianship of the jurist" (*velayat-e faqih*), a controversial concept among Shia scholars that is opposed by Sunnis, who have historically differentiated between political leadership and religious scholarship'. Thus, the all-encompassing and all-pervading division between the Shias and Sunnis has been over the issue of the amalgamation of the 'Political' and 'Religious' which is what the entire regional fracas is all about to a certain extent. The NATO argument too informs us, 'What is to be guarded against is the all pervading expanse and the rise of the state of Iran as a regional power'. The recent lifting of sanctions against NATO has also been a achievement of sorts for President Rouhani who is a reformist and has romped home as the victor in the Iranian Elections with a thumping victory percentage of 57 percent.[6] Arab Spring too brought out Iran into prominence as the various nations were at least symbolically democratized especially in the nations with a Shia majority. Tehran has mobilized the entire Shia communities across the West Asian firmament in order to assist the Government forces in Assad's Syria. Tehran has mobilized various Pakistani and Afghani Shias to take up cudgels against the Assad Regime in Damascus. Thus, apart from the American concern of toppling the applecart of the Islamic State, the Shia Iran's regional influence too remains a cause to be militated against if stability and stolidity has to be reached in the West Asian region. This is the quintessential West Asian dilemma that the United States of America faces in both the short-termish and long-termish ends. President Trump has become the first American President to visit a West Asian nation as one of his initial visits abroad after entering the heady portals of White House. President Trump arrives in Tehran to rebuff the various attempts at policy making by President Obama, when he struck a clearly discernible nuclear deal with Iran and attempted a wholehearted rapprochement between the Shia nation and the 'Satan Nation' as has been the nomenclature used in the generally tardy narrative between both the nations.

The *New York Times* reports, "The Saudis treated him like royalty, with red carpets, lavish meals and American flags flying everywhere. They repeatedly used the word 'historic' to describe his visit, gave him a medal, projected a multistory image of his face on the side of the palatial Ritz-Carlton hotel where he was staying'.[7] It's the spectacle that forms the nascent characteristic of the US Foreign policy that hinges upon larger-than-life antics with the US recently 'missiling' Syria under the rubric of strict reservations being expressed by Russia. The Saudi foreign minister was informed that the Trump administration aims downing extremism and the export of extremism by Tehran, as, related by Secretary of State Rex Tillerson. In summation, the American standpoint in the Houthi conflict in Yemen and the proclamation of an arms deal worth $110 billion with Riyadh happen to be the other frameworks that bring together the twin traditional allies against an Islamic State that breathes its last in the bad lands of Iraq. The December, 2018 developments have spawned a different response in the OSR (Operational Situational Room) as the US Senate has asked the American President to be controlled in its involvement in Yemen which distances the Americans from their Shia ally, Saudi Arabia.

The True-Blue American Regime and the Pre-emptive War

It's a regime of crusading zeal that great powers have always festooned as key part and parcels of their foreign policies and multi-sectoral/sub-regional and extraneous engagements. We are talking about the IR theory facet of 'the Regime' with a convolution of armed and humanitarian interventions that impart the general grandiloquent veneer and visage to the United States of America.[8] It is idealism intertwined with constructivism that defines the Regime Theory, but the United States of America, in its prime vocational veneer underwent an odyssey to intervene and correct the rapacious and distorted trajectories of 'the tedium of growth, development and unison' in nations far removed from its borders where its young and pristine boys have fought wars of attrition and swift manoeuvres in order to live up to the high and anointed values and ideals of the anointed nation. These deserve a mention later in the select narrative. This amounts to a grandiloquent opinion.

No nation can thrive through, in an idealist and Utopian narrative, so the internalities associated with a nation of the order of the United States, too, need to be assimilated as the staple foreign policy narrative of the nation. Henry Kissinger, the American Diplomat, par excellence, has commented in his work,

> Homeland and Domestic concerns too need to be recognized as the parameters of a nation's foreign policy maneuvers and machinations. The American nation's foreign policy is too guided by the idea of populist concerns at home and the domestic welfarist concerns. Thus, the nation too modulates and tapers off its Cruise like Foreign policy missives with the moderating or accentuating influence of its domestic clamourings.[9]

Henry Kissinger has further eulogized and rationalized at both ends, the significance of the Idealist and Liberal notions of doing external relations as initiated by President Woodrow Wilson with his catch phraseology of 'Open Covenants Openly Arrived at', and the themes of self-determination, reparation for the allies along with the attendant notion of free navigation and free trade that were later concretized as post-World War II prescriptions for the larger international system.[10] When the ace American Diplomat raises the question about whether America needs a foreign policy, then it needs to be perceived as the sine qua non of a rhetoric narrative that is so generously festooned with the City of the Shining Hill, that is, United States of America. Of course, the United States of America needs a settled and well-strategized foreign policy that augurs well for the nation in a fast-changing and larger international system that is tom-tommed as a multi-polar mélange and a quintessentially diverse quilt in a post-modern reading of the city on the Canonized Camelot with the daredevil, King Arthur. Thus, the US akin to any great power, is free from a want of a well planned out and panning out foreign policy. The American interventions across the global ecosystem are not part of a rotund and rumbustious outgrowth of an unpruned foreign policy shrubbery. The Bush interventions were too part of a neo-conservative framework of prime time philanthropy that then elicited a universal and liberal Jealousy and the 'Global shying away' from a powerful and capable of helping and aiding, 'Citadel atop a Verdant mountain'. Nothing is unplanned in America, but, interventions gathered a new momentum with the advent of the September 11 catastrophe that caught the American establishment napping. The rationale was now there for the American Seven Seas campaigns with challenging notions as advanced by the West Asian and the larger Third Worldian scapegoats of sovereignty concerns that militated against the so-called rapacious interventions of America. The concerned tale of proliferated ruse was that even the GWOT or, Global War on Terror, against semi-state actors was defended by a cabal of peace suffragettes posing as the custodian of a liberal and humanist world order. American hyperpuissance was disparaged as a pogrom for genocide in the name of gobbling up the natural resources of unsuspecting nations, 'still-to-come-into-their-own'. This ganging up against American wars as intentional neo-imperialistic outages in the name of 'pre-emptive war'[11] was raised as an international hobbyhorse for the Capital Hill that this work attempts to militate against as a biased and a partisan rationale of fashionably castigating the United States of America. It is this staple fare Unionism that PM Modi's Regime in New Delhi as revolted against with strengthening ties with Washington in an, "across-all-spectrums" aspects and perspectives. It may or may not amount to a canny containment of China, but, the policy lays the foundation of closer and profitable ties between a sure New Delhi and a welcoming and positive Washington bringing in allyhood.

The notion of a selfless, self-help foreign policy mechanism does not exist on the face of the real-time Earth, for it to exist, a Utopian world ruled by fairies and Pixies will have to be invented, which does not exist in the jarring note of the real world. Only the Superheroes, can, promptly and with efficient alacrity, make or mar, such a phantasmagorical narrative. A Kal El intervention can make America's day but in a zero-sum-game–ordained international system, the comity of states has to rear string militaries and bust prone economies with a judicious blend of cooperative Regimes and Coalitions in order to sustain as independent and sovereign nations. That's what the American Founding fathers detested, but the 20th-century shenanigans of the International Politics set out to correct that sequestered and isolationist skill set of Capital Hill, though a condescending refrain for America would be the maxim that 'With Great Power comes Great Responsibility', which also serves as a life base line directive from Uncle Ben to Peter Parker in the Spiderman biopic.

Let's shed some light on the notion of Pre-emption in American Foreign Policy thought. The Council on Foreign Relations (CFR) mentions in a report,

Regardless of this definitional question, Stephen Walt points out that

> the attractiveness of both preemptive and preventive war has increased for two reasons. The first reason is functional. The U.S. now has an offensive capability of unmatched versatility and strength. Washington's defense budget for fiscal year 2003 exceeds $450 billion, more than the next 40 countries' military budgets combined. It can deploy its military assets globally and on short-notice to conduct offensive operations.[12]

The renowned IR author, Stephen Walt, writes,

> This military capability provides policymakers with unprecedented military options for preemptive action anywhere in the world. The second reason preemption is more attractive as it stems from the current preponderance of U.S. influence in international affairs. The U.S. faces few political barriers to action. Some states may complain about America as the global bully; but rarely do they counter U.S. power for fear of retribution in other arenas, such as trade, or because of overriding common interests, such as fighting terrorism.[13]

The driving idiom is that, one has to fathom out the differential between being pre-emptive and being preventive. Even, the normalcy-inducing prospect of political legerdemain not involving violence and military, force, can run through as pre-emption, and wars and boots on the ground can also serve as preventive measures to prevent the amplification of a crisis or to ameliorate the popular concerns in a receptacle nation state such as Iraq or Afghanistan. Pre-emption is the genre of conflict resolution that includes a pre-conflict presence of forces and American administrators along with the much needed regular influx of special forces to manage the conflict zones that have weak and struggling defence and counter-terror forces.

What can be safely contended is the notion that Preventive Diplomacy is the nomenclature for the fundamental tenets of US Foreign Policy. One of the avowed zeals of the American foreign policy legerdemain is to prevent and circumvent a war before the conflict takes gargantuan, mammoth and unmanageable proportions in the context of conflict resolution in the myriad panoply of regions and nations spread all across the firmament of the larger international system. One of the supreme creations of the human spirit and the zeitgeist, is, that of grandiloquent prevention. Akin to the hallowed tenet of liberty and equality, it is a seminal concept drawn from a reservoir of optimism that centuries of famines, epidemics and wars have failed to deplete.

A cure in advance with a 'more-than-a-dash' of American prescription is the order of the day and is what the Global Doctor ordered for the entire rubric of the international context. Kevin M Cahill writes in the context of American preventive diplomacy,

> Wanton killing and brutality within supposedly sovereign borders, Ethnic and religious strife, millions of starving or near-to-starving refugees, other millions of migrants fleeing their homes, out for fear for their lives or in a desperate search for a better life, human rights trampled down, appalling poverty in the shadows of extraordinary wealth, inhumanity on an international scale, are some of the awesome challenges which the United States of America and the larger beleaguered nation is confronted with.[14]

Thus, a yeomanly zeal to cut through the alleged façade of interventionism has been festooned upon the general dynamics of the US Foreign Policy. The United States has historically found itself at the cusp of global change and metastasis on more than one occasion that entailed the anointed nation with no other palpable notion but to intervene in besieged nations and strife-torn states. International organizations too have been clinically convened in order to advance the cause of ameliorating the ills of the broken and challenged societies and nations. Societies and nationalities are intertwined terms that posit towards the similar challenges to people and kin in a nation state. As an instance, the UN General Assembly commissioned in 1999, a retrospective analysis of the flawed 'safe haven' policy in Bosnia-Herzegovina adopted by the Security Council.

The Dutch Government has raised a stately commission to consider the circumstances that led to the massacre of 7,000 Moslems in Srebrenica in June 1995.[15] The World Bank should redo the Tito era as to how much largesse was released for ameliorating the shaky economic functionality of the State of Yugoslavia.[16]

All these series of dole-outs that furbished the way of the Yugoslav nation state, without ushering in the checking conditionality such as economic reforms, democratic reform and greater openness, and nations such as Somalia, which were intervened upon by the United States, too need to be fairly documented. Thus, before castigating and labelling the foreign policy of the United States, as, being hegemonic and crassly interventionist, the larger issues of having 'no other option' and the theme of not letting the impoverished and challenged populations suffer have emerged as the cornerstone of the American Foreign Policy thought, proclivities and proactivity. The intent to ameliorate the ills of the world should not be equated with crassly national interest and realistically ordained system of the grandiloquent American Foreign Policy. The American intent has been fashionably questioned in the larger context of the American context of pre-emptive war and the attendant notion of Preventive Diplomacy. The acerbic and volatile, politically motivated and Campus-spawned attacks on the intent of the US Diplomacy have been wrongly cocooned in a left-liberal narrative that militates against remotely connected to the American nation. It's always been a manicheastic attempt on the so called vile and interventionist skill set of US Diplomacy.

The early warning effectiveness of the American state and the larger structure of the International Organizations, too, have been a matter of deliberations and organizational finesse related to intelligence gathering. The capacity to collect and disseminate information on the emerging crisis has vastly increased since the mid-1980s, due to computing and electronic developments. Early warning as field monitoring is a modicum of Preventive Diplomacy. This field method is a long-established mechanism that the on-the-ground civil societal instrumentalities along with nation state actors through their diplomats have attempted since the advent of the 'Conflict'. The US Foreign Service bureaucracy is no exception to the rule. In the context of the United States, the Office for the Coordination of Humanitarian Affairs' Humanitarian Early Warning System was designed in 1991, with the idea of early warning being in the mind. It consists of an electronic database of statistical indicators on more than a 100 nations along with headlines on recent political, humanitarian and other developments in a small number of countries.[17] Thus, the initial spurt has to come from the intelligence agencies and the Homeland Security Department turf, which is part of the national security and the crisis prevention aspects of the American Diplomacy. Humanitarian disasters occur in localized milieus, and in the want of an effective crisis resolution team in the hallowed portals of the United Nations, the much castigated Capitol Hill has had to take a call repeatedly in the context of conflict negotiations and larger nation building.

Apart from the quintessential places and strategic stations, where the United States has intervened, one can take as an interlude, the instantciations of the American interest in the all-significant nation centre of People's Republic of China. With the entry of President Trump in the White House, the Chinese expect a strangulation with the Xingxiang and the Taiwanese themes too coming into a diplomatic and strategic play. The Trump Doctrine of blaming the Han and the flippant Dragon for the issues and malpractices of subsidies and currency manipulations leads to a great ordeal for Beijing, but, after the art of playing the standard blame game on a recalcitrant Beijing, if President Donald J. Trump does not act decisively against China, then he may run the danger of being branded as a paper tiger.[18]

The much followed and commented upon visit of the American Secretary of State, Rex Tillerson, to Beijing sets the tone and the tenor for the expected tête-à-tête between President Donald J Trump and President Xi Xingping at Florida in the United States in the month of April in 2017.

The Rex Factor: How a New America Engages the Talloned Dragon?

Is it that the American foreign policy rigmarole has decided to go beyond the idea of a Euro-centric world that has already taken a backseat with Rex Tillerson skipping his NATO meet and meeting the Chinese counterpart of President Trump? The state of the nation is in a secure station as China intends to take up the pedestal left across by the American machine, as President Trump's era of protectionism and inward-looking exclusivity, is, on an upswing with the American nation pandered away from the TPP agreement, which was one of the bow-tie events of the Obama Administration. Can the dragon panda take over the positioning of a higher moral ground from a receding, but, not dwindling United States of America? PRC is the second largest bulwark economy of the international system that is a fact of World Politics, which cannot be relegated to the backburner despite qualms by the liberals. Also, with the Chinese-communist crackdown on the artists, writers, freedom sayers and the proponents of dissidence and freedom of speech and expression, the American and that too Trump's role playing in China assumes greater strategic significance. It would be interesting to note that how a new America that thrives on 'Open spaces' deals with a closed PRC and its numerously quoted dissidents in an age of open convergence.

The Tillerson visit can have other ramifications, too, which are worthy of note. As an instance, the American theme of regulating the North Korean nuclear dreams and the ballistic missile tests being unearthed by Pyongyang happen to be the erstwhile issues amounting to Asia-Pacific regionalism. The

White House through Sean Spicer has already declared, 'The options of leveraging military action against North Korea cannot be completely ruled out as the nation has dangerous and unregulated nuclear ambitions with the reach of one of its ICBMs to reach over all across to the American homeland/ mainland. An assault over the North Korean intent cannot be ruled out'. Thus, the American withdrawal from the Obama's hobbyhorse of the TPP might be one transformation in the US Foreign Policy thought, but the strategic and geo-political objectives to remedy the nuclear ills of North Korea are to be set to be met by the White House. Also, the Chinese disdain and curtailment of the Chinese dissidents since the Tiananmen square incident have been the pet issues with the White House. It is here that this human rights access has been utilized to beat the Chinese back. Also, going along with the global and humanist world view of rule of law, constitutionalism and democracy, the Chinese-communist regime has been found wanting on many fronts, which the American philanthropic interest has raised voices against. The fear of incarceration in the Chinese mainland along with the dampening interest among the Chinese for the crucial political and economic reforms, have, left much to be cleaned on the Chinese internal slate that is anyway hidden beyond an iron veil.

The mellowing down of President Trump has truly occurred that brings to the fore, the, idiom that candidate Trump's campaign trail and the bombast was only meant to polarize the votes and the President once in the seat of power would begin in a true-blue Globally acceptable and elitist-politically correct fashion. President Trump, time and again, led the American charge against the Sinic state on various counts finally hinting at New Delhi's utility against the rising clout of People's Republic of China. But, the Russian side seems to have taken over with the American President Trump castigating the Moscovites of wiretapping the Trump tower and other Republican Party bases. Then, where does the Chinese significance stand? Rex Tillerson has displayed a complete intolerance for the inimical ambitions of Pyongyang with the Chinese as a kind of registered protests. The North Koreans have timed the test of a certain type of Rocket Engine at the Sohae missile testing site with the visit of American Secretary of State, Rex Tillerson, and his subsequent meeting with the Chinese Premier, Xi Jinping. The entire Korean Peninsula seems to be challenged and imbalanced as of now with the South Korean Premier too under pressure of being harangued under graft and nepotism charges as is evident from the mass protests being witnessed in Seoul and other parts of

South Korea. Still, come 2018 and the Daredevil Summitry between the North Korean Premier and President Trump seems to have drawn the world back from a conflictual brink and warring doldrums. No clear cut timelines were spawned but the immediate threat of a n Armageddon was surefootedly relegated to the backburner in the 2018 Summitry.

The Cable News Network (CNN) has reported,

> Both the nations agreed there are opportunities for greater cooperation between China and the United States, but acknowledged there are, and will be in the future, differences between the two countries. Trump is anticipating that the heads of States, of both the nations will soon be able to meet face to face for discussions that will chart the course for future US-China relations.[19]

Thus, the issue of compromise, camaraderie, bonhomie and mutual trust and cooperation in the bilateral relationship has been highlighted in the relationship between both the nations of the order of United States of America and the People's Republic of China. These homilies came out as part of the declared "agreement byte" between Washington and Beijing. These words shed all the important light on the theme of renunciation of enmity between both the nations though the Tillerson chemistry cannot rule out the entire utilitarian nature of New Delhi's role as a tool to balance a stately Beijing. CNN has further reported that 'China is Pyongyang's only major global ally, with bilateral trade accounting for 70 percent of North Korea's total trade, providing a political and economic lifeline to Kim's increasingly isolated regime. Trump has repeatedly called on Beijing to use its leverage over its unpredictable neighbor'. President Trump and no longer the President elect, has, ably pointed out to Beijing's mandarins. President Trump tweeted, 'North Korea is behaving very badly. They have been "playing" the United States for years. China has done little to help'![20] Secretary of State, Rex Tillerson, met the Chinese Foreign Minister Wang Yi, and emphasized the 'renewed determination' by Beijing and Washington to 'work together to convince the North Korean government to choose a better path and a different future for its people'. Though the February 2019 talks in Hanoi have faltered.

The significance of the Chinese overarch too cannot be ruled out as the Han nation under the talons of a strangulating regime balances power in the South China Sea disputes. It's also interesting to note that as part of the standard American strategy, US and New Delhi are hands in gloves in tackling the

Chinese talons from swooping down on the maritime space decks in the sphere of the Indian Ocean rim nations. Rex Tillerson is the 69th American Secretary of State, an energy executive, a civil engineer and a diplomat who has a background in owning energy companies with an involvement of Russia. That was beyond the point, as, being a head chaperoning the Americans, he needed to chart out a smart trajectory for the United States in an energy acquisition market that is equally and effectively populated by Beijing. The American Secretary of State also needs to keep in mind that Washington was castigated in the past in the context of West Asia and Iraq that US marines and the high-tech military equipment stampeded inside nations such as Iraq and Afghanistan on the Kuwaiti issue and the weapons of mass destruction (WMDs) allegation.Still, when it came to the standpoints of the North Korean Premier, Kim Jong Un, the Americans relied on 'other nation-diplomacy', in order to tackle the bug bear of the North Korean Communist Panopticon. Here, the Americans relied upon standard Diplomatic methods averse to the militarist approach in West Asia. This is the key transformation reflected in the Trump's real politick that the American Secretary of State had to convey to and emphasize upon the Chinese Premier to play out the grand balance of power (BoP) and the astute gaming act.

The Nationalist China: The Trump–Jinping Ping-Pong Set-Piece

No nation ought to have a two-nation theory, as, it militates against the founding myth of a race, its people and the nation. India with its own two-nation theory suffered the rites of partition and ungainly carnage. The Mainland China and the outgrowth of its self-same body organic in the form of Taiwan, too, militates against the rationale of a nation state, ideally speaking. The schism between the communist supremo Mao Tse Tung and the flight of Chiang Kai Shek leading the Kuomintang[21] happens to be a perennial scar on the founding myth of the Chinese nation but Taiwan too needs its independence. The small north-top nation of Taiwan has followed a capitalist and democratic mode of development and is a micro-scab tissue on the organic scaffolding of China according to the Mainland China's argument. The Chinese never gave up on the severed Taiwan while the status of Taiwan has always been mired in the quicksand twilight zone of Taiwan's rights and status. The smaller administrative unit with its promiscuity with the United States soon charted a grand growth and development story for itself. Also, in the contemporary context, President Trump's post-inaugural conversation with the state head in

Taiwan led to a blowback with the Beijing, where-in, the old wounds, despite a Nixon–Mao détente in 1971, as, part of Ping-Pong Diplomacy, were sure to make an impact upon the general tenor of the Washington–Beijing bilateral.

The Taiwan Relations Act (TRA) passed in April 1979[22] declared substantial but non-diplomatic relations with the people and the nation of Taiwan. Senator Barry Goldwater and other members of the Congress opposed the decision of President Jimmy Carter, as he had abrogated the Taiwan-US Mutual Defence Pact that has served as a larger security umbrella for Taiwan since 1954. The Chinese act of supporting Washington in its role-playing in Afghanistan and the dreary Dragon's expedition against Vietnam, the sore for America, brought Beijing and United States together for a brief furlough. Thus, as a fallout of this rift in the American homeland, the Institution of the order of the American Institute in Taiwan was established that spawned new commercial and abiding cultural ties between United States and the ROC, Republic of China. The American understanding leaves apart the islands other than the mainland Taiwanese island and the Penghu island away from the jurisdiction of the TRA passed in 1979. The purport of the TRA happens to be historically, 'The Taiwan Relations Act potentially requires the U.S. to intervene militarily if the PRC attacks or invades Taiwan'. The act states that 'The United States will make available to Taiwan such defence articles and defence services in such quantity, as, may be necessary to enable Taiwan to maintain sufficient self-defence capabilities. However, the decision about the nature and quantity of defence services that America will provide to Taiwan, is to be determined by the President and Congress'.[23] United States has displayed a strategic ambivalence in the context of Taiwan in order to tread the twin canoe-balancing act on the Oriental seas of the Asiatic Space. It is this development and snippet out of Illinois that has to be sorted out peacefully by the involved nation state actors.

Initially, in the contemporary context, President Trump had called for a review of the status of ROC, but after a conversation with Beijing akin to other issues such as immigration policy and others, he has mellowed down a great deal. The *New York Times* reports,

> Even though Trump has said he will support the 'One China' policy, China cannot fully trust him, said Yan Xuetong, dean of the school of international relations at Tsinghua University, in Beijing. 'Even his own people don't trust him'.[24]

Thus, the Washington folks need to stick to a tough talking position if they seemingly want to appear to be stately like. Still, a softening down in the light of Xi Jinping's strong observations on the American standpoint has been taken in astutely by President Trump's, "uppity" and upbeat campaign trail and the subsequent Presidency. The question that needs to be answered and ruminated upon happens to be, 'can the twin superpowers share power in the Pacific'? The American stratagem towards PRC has always been interpreted as being that of strategic ambiguity and one that of 'cooperative competition' in nearly all contested terrains in the larger international system including the nationalist northern speck over China. To put to rest doubts about any American legerdemain, President Trump reiterated the American support to a 'One China Policy' in a telephonic conversation with the Chinese Premier Xi Jinping.[25]

It might be a tactical retreat by the American strategists and President Trump. The CNN in one of the news reports informs the audience, 'President Trump's willingness to pull back from some of his more extreme ideas has been welcomed by market watchers. The pledge to Xi on Taiwan '"matters to investors because if China can bring about a change like this, it may succeed in softening other U.S. policy positions", said Paul Donovan, global chief economist at UBS Wealth Management'. The Chinese are of the opinion, pragmatically speaking, that Beijing is hopeful about the United States mellowing down and taking substantial interest in the trade negotiations between both the nations. Still, when China refers to the right of self-determination and insurgent ministrations in provinces such as Xinjiang, its own standpoint in the context of a twilight-zone Taiwan stands on shaky grounds and in a translucent twilight zone. The new Chinese Policy of 'leapfrog development' happens to be that of serving the mainframe Han race as most of the demographic alterations in the sphere of internal migrations have already been accomplished. Thus, the Chinese canard of playing the aggressed-upon nation in the context of Taiwan, falls flat in the light of the strife-torn East-Turkistan movement. The Uighur Turks were the original ethnic group, which were belittled in all prevalent manners in order to hike the fortunes of mainland unity, the Han way as the Chinese call it as part of mainland, "Chinese Dream". The same discrimination gets reflected in the manner in which national day parades exist as charades in light of the pattern of 'select participation at national events'. So much the so for the Chinese doublespeak. Also, the initiation of CPEC on India's western frontiers is another reflection of Chinese hegemony as MEA shifting achieved China's Neutrality in Pulwama episode on 14th February 2019. US has always had a positive terror response mechanism.

The newspaper *Guardian* has reported that China has reiterated in January, 2017 very categorically that Taiwan is non-negotiable. Thus, the entire alternate way of lifers can echo the separatist question than China's persistent insistence harping on an arcane conception of national unison needs to be recalibrated in a liberal paradigm of universalism and omniscience of the 'milk of human kindness'. This allows dissent and freedom of existence in the name of the Taiwanese insistence on self-determination. Even, going by national polls in Taiwan, most of the Taiwanese nationals prefer a separate existential streak for themselves and do not prefer to kow-tow along with the Dragonwing's flippancy. President Trump does not propose to utilize the Taiwanese angle as a bargaining chip to outdo PRC diplomatically in the Asia Pacific. In return for the Chinese demands, the United States of America has already raised the bogey of the North Korean question that insists on making Pyongyang retract from its scary and regimental nuclear ambitions and the ambiguities associated with it. The American concerns over North Korea are genuine as it has ratcheted up the threat to take the military route over North Korea but China, too, has alertly refuted the American threats and concerns. Still, as a summation, the Trump dispensation can hope for a negotiated settlement with Beijing in the peninsular region, if, not with the North Korean Dictator. Still, Chinese currency manipulation and subsidies serve as the constant obstructions in the steady streaming of Sino–US relations. Also, Washington should link up its 'Rebalancing' with Asia in the light of the Chinese claims over Taiwan. Thus, a yet to be undertaken intervention by the United States inside the vestigial territoriality of PRC, can serve as a metaphor for American stealth, pelf, power, diplomatic and defence interventionism that might become a reality if the Chinese torment the archipelago nation states in and near the South China Seas too much and if the scenario in the Taiwanese waters deteriorates a great deal in the light of the Chinese rejection of the International Tribunal vis-à-vis the fate and the legal status of the nation state of the micro Northtip state of Taiwan. Thus, the question which can be conveniently asked is that can the entire International system and the bland Asiatic Space expect an American intervention in the name of China and North Korea akin to the American intrusion in Iraq in the name of the status of WMDs and the fate of Israel? Definitely, what transpired in Iraq and Afghanistan is quaintly different from the Orient's touché with United States as the oil and other sectarian factors are not present in the Asiatic situation room.

The American Presidency and the surrounding power paraphernalia is a spectacle in itself. The US constitution empowers the President to act as the final Commander-in-Chief of the American system along with being the Chief executive Official of the nation. Myriad hallowed and larger-than-life Presidents have illuminated the portals of the White House that itself was destroyed by the British in 1815. Thus emanates the norm of insecurity, and dilemmas despite the mammoth pelf and strength of the American dream. Still, the American expanse through its external interventions has reemphasized the notion of American stealth, power and strategic girth. Why doesn't US intervene in India? The simpleton response is that both the nations believe in the fundamentals of rule of Law, constitutionalism, liberalism along with the proud dictum of democracy. These are the dictums and nation life blood principles that have been declared as being too trite homilies and hackneyed syllogisms, which only amount to nebulous political theory precepts. Still, a mainstream scholar would know that these nations are the ones that are gelled by these seemingly hackneyed dictums that are life principles for the hoi polloi of these nations, their establishments and their socio-cultural and economic oeuvres. Let's take a dekko inside the Indian and American tango before one goes into the so-called intrusive interventions of the American nation peppered with blithe adjectives describing the so-called interventionist and the so-called illegal nature of American moves in the larger international system!

Since its independence and much before that, India espoused the cause célèbre of anti-colonialism and anti-imperialism with the apt push to emanate from President Franklin Delano Roosevelt. President Roosevelt, the differently abled leader, communicated to London to grant independence to India as per the Fourteen hallowed points of President Woodrow Wilson. President Wilson also enumerated the right to self-determination and the notion of open covenants openly arrived at. Thus, since the early times the American ideals of liberty, fraternity, justice and rule of law, became part of the formalized framework of American Presidency. As time progressed, some of the standpoints of White House could not gel palpably with its high moral perch and anointed pitching globally.

One significant signpost of the India–US bilateral relationship was defined by the generous and India-centric role played by President John F Kennedy after India faced major military reverses in on 19 November 1962. JFK, the much loved head of state, alerted the American forces stationed in Philippines and offered aid to New Delhi. During JFK's times, there was a massive increment in economic aid to India, unrelated to the China war. There was talk of arms sale to India in the American Press and General Ayub Khan on his Mount Vernon visit in 1961, began to feel disillusioned with the American tilt towards India. President Kennedy also met Ayub Khan and their "mutual love of horses" became popular and as Peshawar was the required base for the U-2 flights over Soviet Union, so the Americans could not completely negate Islamabad. The role played by Zulfikar Ali Bhutto in the US–Sino détente too made the White House's initial tilt towards Pakistan to concretize as a significant policy option. It was the Ping-Pong diplomacy carried on by President Nixon in 1971 that furthered the distance between India and United States and the American factor helped strengthen the 'all-weather friend' status of the Sino-Pakistan partnership in the quintessential mould of the Cold war. Who can forget the gunboat diplomacy ushered in by Henry Kissinger and President Nixon? With the passage of the Nuclear Non-Proliferation Act in the seventies, President Gerald Ford discontinued the supply of nuclear fuel to the Tarapur Atomic Power Station (TAPS) that sowed seeds of discord in the relationship between both the nations and was straightened to some extent by the acquiescence of President Ronald Reagan in ascertaining the supply of nuclear fuel to Tarapur.

Still, as a parallel to the positivity with the TAPS, it was during the tenure of President Reagan, India was asked to seek a new source for the low enriched uranium and to adopt the International Atomic Energy Agency (IAEA) safeguards and to follow the mixed fuel route that was rejected by Sethna as part of the Indian delegation to Washington in 1981. President Bill Clinton played the role of a Nuclear Ayatollah, where, it was demanded of India to sign the paper on the nuclear non-proliferation regime. It was Clinton only who imposed sanctions on the New Delhi's May 1998 Nuclear tests when the Buddha smiled for a second time in Pokhran. In fact during a visit to India during 1998, the American interlocutor, Strobe Talbott, communicated the intent of President Clinton to Jaswant Singh that Washington wanted New Delhi to sign the Comprehensive Test Ban Treaty. Thus, right from President Gerald Ford's times to President George Bush, Jr, Washington did several strategic flip-flops vis-à-vis and nuclear relations between both the nations. It was with the signing of the 123 nuclear agreement that Washington amended its law in order to create a leeway for India to avail of the Civil-Nuclear deal despite India being home to nuclear weapons and militarization of nuclear power. Thus, despite the sea of criticism, which headed the way of President George Bush, Jr, after the US intervention in Iraq and Afghanistan, the India–US nuclear deal was a tangible achievement in the relationship ushered in by President George Bush Jr., President Clinton too warned the Pakistan Prime Minister, Mian Nawaz Shareef, on 4 July 1999 that if Islamabad did not withdraw its camouflaged forces from Kargil, then Washington might be forced to shift its emphasis to New Delhi. This threat worked and hundreds of lives on both the warring sides were saved.

President Obama narrated the Gandhian hymn in New Delhi when he visited when he crooned, 'Abide with me, fast falls the eventide'. President Obama had contended that South Asia is not a region on "a short fuse" but the India–US partnership is the new defining partnership of the current age that is much more premised upon soft power and economic diplomacy. President Obama and the Indian PM Narendra Modi strengthened the mutual cooperation on climate change and energy and defence cooperation was solidified between both the nations, with President Obama registering governmental and corporate reservations about the civil nuclear liability legislation, which augments the accident and compensatory liability during nuclear plant accidents on the American investors. President Trump will further cement the ties with Prime Minister Modi with the enunciation of his verbiage-infested but spectacularly effective and practical idiom of revisiting American homeland, trade, war strategy and geo-economic partnerships in the near neighbourhood and the larger world system. In a post Pulwama scenario, President Trump has reined in a Rogue Pakistan.

Thus, the India–US partnership is practically premised on democratic divisiveness, which is impacted upon by the vagaries of the ever-changing and anarchic international system. To expect an American President to follow a continuity in tandem with a State framework and with the ideals of the American founding myth would be too much of an ask in a fragile global ecosystem. The American Founding myth also incorporates the idiom of expanding the hackneyed but morally high-grounded edifice of global morality, peacenik behaviour, constitutionalism and rule of law all amalgamated by the gel of liberal democracy. These amount to American interventionism. This expanse inside the organic whole of the world system requires both tangible (military and territorial) and intangible interventions (through Soft power) that need to be disseminated studiously and assiduously if the altercasting[26] and the mirror image spawning of a neo-Liberal world has to be festooned upon the larger international system. It is the identity role-playing that is significant here, which notoriously embalms a negativity oriented chutzpah over the United States of America, which needs to carve out a novae 'identity theory' about itself that only presents the United States in a positive, a dedicatedly hallowed light and a benign halo. The new liberal 'identity theory'[27] ought to spawn a benign narrative out of the United States and its attendant Dream and spare itself the spreadeaglism of a superstate but a nation with an avowed zeal to reform and regulate the world with its benign and strictly legal interventions. The American expanse in the tormented and the besmirched regions and nations of the world, deserves a greater re look and a revisitation. Still, as a first in the India-US relationship, the National Security Strategy unveiled by President Trump, accepts India as a rising Diva on the international stage and intends that India ought to take up a leadership role in Asia and other larger regions of the world as a riposte to the advent of Chinese dream and its attendant base and superstructure. This is all the more important in the light of Pakistan Sponsored Pulwama massacre that India asserts itself like US did at the beginning of the 20th century.

NOTES

1. *The Guardian*, February 2017.
2. *The New York Times*, February 2017.
3. *The Indian Express*, 4 March 2017.
4. Osnos, Evan, 'The Gathering storm of protests Against Term', *The New Yorker*, 17 November 2016.
5. Council on Foreign Relations, 'The Sunni-Shia Divide'. https://www.cfr.org/peace-conflict-and-human-rights/sunni-shia-divide/p33176#!/p33176. Accessed 17 May 2017.
6. *The Indian Express*, 21 May 2017.
7. *The New York Times*, 21 May 2017.
8. Keohane, Robert O., 'The Demand for International Relations', *International Organizations*, 36 (2), 1982, pp. 325–355.
9. Kissinger, H., *Does America need a Foreign Policy: Toward a Policy of the 21st century*, New York: Simon and Schuster, 2002, pp. 1–22.
10. Kissinger, H., *Diplomacy*, New York: Simon and Schuster, 1995, pp. 30–45.
11. Council on Foreign Relations, 'The Bush Doctrine's Doctrine of Preemption: When, how and Where'? http://www.cfr.org/world/bush-administrations-doctrine-preemption-prevention-/p6799. Accessed 19 March 2017.
12. Reiter, D., 'Exploding The Powder Keg Myth: Preemptive Wars Almost Never Happen', *International Security*, 20(2), 1995, pp. 5–34.
13. Council For American Relations, 'The Bush Doctrine's Doctrine of Preemption: When, how and Where.' http://www.cfr.org/world/bush-administrations-doctrine-preemption-prevention-

/p6799. Accessed 28 March 2017.

14. Cahill, Kevin M., *Introduction to: Preventive Diplomacy: Stopping Wars Before They Start*, New York: Routledge, 2000, pp. 1–10.
15. Honig, J.W. and Norbert Booth, *Srebrenica: Record of a War Crime*, London: Penguin, 1996.
16. Ibid.
17. Cahill, op. cit., pp. 250–255.
18. *The New York Times*, March 2017.
19. CNN Report Transcript, 14 March 2017.
20. President Donald J Trump's twitter account.
21. Snow, E., '*Red Star Over China*, Perseus Books, 1994.
22. HR 2479: Taiwan Relations Act, 96th Congress (1979-1980). https://www.congress.gov/bill/96th-congress/house-bill/2479. Accessed 12 April 2017.
23. Ibid.
24. *The New York Times*, April 2017.
25. Ibid.
26. Wendt, Alexander, 'Anarchy is What States Make of it: The Social Construction of Power Politics', *International Organizations*, 46 (2), 1992, pp. 391–425.
27. Ibid.

2

The First Contact: The Spanish War

THE Mayflower Pact and the arrival of the Spaniards on the Florida Coast and sections of the East Coast have been evocatively described in the work, *The Epic of America.* This spawning of the new world can be termed as the 'first contact Intervention' in the United States of America with the Aztecs and the Incas. The history books relate to us, 'The Americans watched as beyond the craggy hills, the ships marooned on the coast with the white visitors both exchanging gifts with the nomads and the Aztecs and also massacring the local denizens at times in the tropical pasturelands of America'. Still, if one delves inside the true vortex of legalia, then, one can surf asunder how the United States since the dying days of the 19th century decided to end its days of isolation and grandiloquent sequestration after the American preparation to festoon itself over the international system was complete and the girth of germination was accomplished. Also, the American Epic could only be penned evocatively after the nation had balanced itself in the aftermath of the divisive, but, equally unifying Civil War. The American spat with Spain in the Hearst News chain wars in Mexico in 1898 can be counted as the second American intervention that was enlivened by the American print Media. The owner of the Hearst News chain of newspapers gave a clarion call to his war correspondents to cover the American war with Spain, and the consequential war cry of 'You give me the pictures, I will give you the war'.[1]

The American Public Broadcasting Service reports,

> In 1898, Hearst chartered the yacht Sylvia to Cuba to witness battles between the U.S. Navy and the Spanish Fleet. From his ship, Hearst continued to publish sensationalist stories in a "Cuban Edition",

> personally making sure that the U.S. public stayed informed. After the Spanish-American War, Hearst remained an outspoken and powerful member of the U.S. press. Hearst was critical of the treatment of U.S. troops as they returned home and blasted the Secretary of War, Russell A. Alger.[2]

Such was the labelled and initial tirades of management during an initial American foray for strengthening and cementing the American nation as a near–to-neophytic state coming into its own. The entire war-making exercise was akin to deft Media management but the service that the Hearst Chain rendered to the American nation, was, that of positing the American striving of strengthening the territorial station of the nation. Also, it was a reiteration of the all popular and steady Monroe Doctrine that signalled to the European conquistadors that the North American sphere was solely an American dominion. This media military and Industry complex was to become the driving idiom and a stultifying anachronism for the enemies of America.

The Hearst Chain of national dailies in the United States during the turning days of the 19th century made the entire American nation rally around the flag, which is a predominant phenomenon in the American nation and the attendant homeland. The nation of immigrants, that is, United States of America, was growing territorially and as an alleged usurper nation as claimed by the alternate way of lifers. The old-world elan of a Eurocentric world was pitted against the new-world verve and panache of the American settlers, where-in, the contested territory in the American south became everyone's pet peeve with America embarking about a strengthening of territoriality. The US–Spanish war resulted in the ending of dominions of the Spaniards in the Americas and the rise in unparalleled influence by the Americans in Western Pacific and Latin America.

The American History website informs,

> Spain announced an armistice on April 9 and speeded up its new program to grant Cuba limited powers of self-government, but the U.S. Congress soon afterward issued resolutions that declared Cuba's right to independence, demanded the withdrawal of Spain's armed forces from the island, and authorized the President's use of force to secure that withdrawal while renouncing any U.S. design for annexing Cuba.[3]

Thus, the future of the regional history would pit the American nation in a perennial battle of ideologies and national life patterns with Cuba, but, here was a turn of century war that pitted the United State's establishment against the Spanish nation in favour and support of Cuba and its rebels that was later on to earn the American sobriquet of a recalcitrant nation state. Thus, the blame game that portrays the United States as a hegemon and a bully has to be redone globally as in the context of the US–Spanish war, US stood with the rebels and the conquistadors in the form of the Spanish nation. The blame nomenclature of impounding the US with the appellation of being a neo-imperialistic power does not stand scrutiny as it was in the context of the US–Spanish war, the Americans were found with the 'Right guys'.

The History Channel further reports,

> By the Treaty of Paris (signed Dec. 10, 1898), Spain renounced all claim to Cuba, ceded Guam and Puerto Rico to the United States, and transferred sovereignty over the Philippines to the United States for $20,000,000. The Spanish-American War was an important turning point in the history of both antagonists. Spain's defeat decisively turned the nation's attention away from its overseas colonial adventures and inward upon its domestic needs, a process that led to both a cultural and a literary renaissance and two decades of much-needed economic development in Spain. The victorious United States, on the other hand, emerged from the war a world power with far-flung overseas possessions and a new stake in international politics that would soon lead it to play a determining role in the affairs of Europe.[4]

Thus, the war with Spain waged by the United States can be earmarked as the novel instance of the initiation of the 'American Manifest Destiny' ' that relied upon the strengthening of its territorial expanse along with symbolically positing the military and geo-economic superiority of the American nation, as, per the sentiment of the Monroe Doctrine that was the notion of an 'America-led exclusivity'. This supreme pedestal of power and pelf with a decidedly healthy bargaining positioning in the global arena was to be attained by cementing the internal stolidity of the American homeland. Thus, the US after the days of civil war (1860–64) and the attendant Big Business era of modernity and industrialization and the populist-progressive movement had embarked on a preparatory time period of isolation to engage the larger international system from a more powerful and well-accoutred power perch. The instance of the US–Spanish war was a symbolic showcasing of the notion that the United States had arrived on the international scene. This was a process ascertained much later by the efforts of President Woodrow Wilson, who, was one of the framers of the League of Nations (LoN), which could not reach fruition due to certain interposing reasons. Who can forget the notion of the 'lengthening shadows of the empty chair left waiting for the American representative'[5] in the council of the LoN. Thus, the American odyssey as a grandiloquent redeemer nation of the World, had begun with this Hearst News chain war, if it can be nomenclatured that way. Thus, the American absence in the LoN was cited as one of the key reasons as to why the American nation had become an indispensable point of reference for the entire international system with the Washington's role of spreading good messages[6] about global norm setting and its largely peacenik role felt loud and clear by the Global comity of nations.

The US–Spanish war ushered in the dawn of the new American century with epochal proportions. Ivan Musicant writes in the work on American History, *Empire by Default,*

> This is a full and clear account of the war, balanced in viewpoint and meticulous in detail. M. describes the details of the Cuban rebellion up to '98. The author notes the strengths and weaknesses of the various personalities. Taking his departure from Jackson Turner on the end of the frontier, he holds that the outward venture of the U.S. was inevitable. Since so many have dealt with the journalistic side, M. need not stress it. A prominent role was played by racism in the tendency to withdraw support from the Cuban rebels. The full American panorama can be unearthed in the spheres of political and military aspects.[7]

On reading the engaging work on American history, one can note the tenor of war in 1899 that had a generous sprinkling of the War veterans leading the war against a conquistading Spain. Ivan Musicant writes,

> One interesting feature was the role of Civil War veterans, including Generals who were Generals then: Joe Wheeler, once C.S.A.; from the U.S.A.: Miles, Merritt, Schofield, Dodge, and others who were field officers during the rebellion. Dewey's hero was Farragut, whom he not only idolized, but also emulated, combining careful preparation with the courage to join battle. These men provided links to the soldiers of WWI and later.[8]

Thus, the military and the inward-strengthening nature of the American homeland and its girth is brought forth by this grand narrative, where-in, the

United States had taken the first 'dithering and baby steps' towards an odyssey of emerging as a Superman and a stand-out but not stand-alone Global power in the larger international firmament. The war is also known as the 'Splendid Little War' where-in both the nations of the order of US and Spain, were being directed by the internal conditionalities of security and politics in their respective homelands that were conditions directly related to the American war effort in 1898. The idiom of the attack on USS Maine has been studied by the Naval Historians, where-in, the tipping point for Washington was considered to be the attack on the US Naval warship, USS Maine.

Trumbull White writes in his historical account of the US–Spanish war,

> Information concerning the island of Cuba has been of an exceedingly unsatisfactory character until the search"light of American inquiry was thrown upon it from the beginning of the war for Cuban liberty early in 1895. Although our next"door neighbor to the south, with a perfect winter climate and a host of interesting and picturesque attractions for travelers, tourists had been comparatively few, measured by the numbers that might have been expected. All of the reasons for this were those which naturally followed the characteristic Spanish rule of the island.[9]

The author then pinpoints at the strangulation of the public sphere and rights of the Cuban people as the Spanish rule over Cuba and others was very arcane and archaic in nature with the *vox populi* being besmirched by the dictatorial denomination of the Spanish Regime in Cuba. The author writes,

> Publicity was not welcomed, inquiry was not welcomed, travelers were not welcomed. The cities and the accommodations they offered were in many ways far behind those of like age and size in the other countries of the globe. Railway construction and the making of highways had lagged disgracefully, because the exorbitant taxes collected were looted by the officers of the government as their own spoils. No other country so near to the highways of ocean commerce and so accessible from the United States was so little known.[10]

Here, the author brings out the tyrannical nature of the Spanish Regime with the high-handed suppression being practiced by the Spanish denomination in Cuba. The American perception rightly portrays the demeaned plight of the Cubans who were actually foraying on for their freedom of livelihood and expression and were reflecting dissent with the alien and European rule of the Spaniards. The pictorial portrayals of the US–Spanish war also led to the development of the military histories of the American war operations of the genre of land, naval and diplomatic aspects in the context of the US–Spanish war. It was definitively a test case for the floating of the seething current of American power but not a marketing of the new weaponry and warring techniques in the light of other interventions by Pentagon.

It was not a crass case of a stolid American intervention, but the excessive repression being unleashed by the Cuban Regimes, such as Valeriano Weyler, caused the idiom of 'Freedom for Cuba' to gain traction and sympathy for the Cuban cause.Unlike some present day conflicts and responses to it, the American establishment responded handsomely. David Trask writes in the Library of Congress publication,

> The Cuban cause gained increasing support in the United States, leading President Grover Cleveland to press for a settlement, but instead Spain sent General Valeriano Weyler to pacify Cuba. His stern methods, including reconcentration of the civilian population to deny the guerrillas support in the countryside, strengthened U.S. sympathy for the Cubans. President William McKinley then increased pressure on Spain to end the affair, dispatching a new minister to Spain for this purpose.[11]

The author further writes about the early military successes of the American Navy that belittled the standpoint of the Spanish frigates, The war began with two American successes. Admiral William Sampson immediately established a blockade of Havana that was soon extended along the north coast of Cuba and eventually to the south side. Sampson then prepared to counter Spanish effort to send naval assistance. Then, on 1 May, Commodore George Dewey, commanding the Asiatic Squadron, destroyed Admiral Patricio Montoyo's small force of wooden vessels in Manila Bay. Dewey had earlier moved from Japan to Hong Kong to position himself for an attack on the Philippines.[12]

Apart from gaining Cuban freedom and independence, President McKinley too aimed at negotiating the annexation of Puerto Rico and Philippines.It was finally the thrust of the American land forces gathered in the county of Tampa in Florida that managed the help arriving from mainland Spain blockading the sea fronts. Thus, it rendered telling body-blows to the already present Spanish Armada along with the help coming the way of the Spanish mainland. The American contiguity to Cuba proved to be a telling factor apart from the succor received from the land forces gathered in Southern

America. Several historians have opined that the emergence of America in the international firmament was ascertained much later during the World War I, but the idea of the supremacy as 'the Global Power' was expressed pithily as the American naval and land operations too stretched in areas such as Manila in Philippines and Santiago. They finally tilted the balance of the battle towards the United States of America and President McKinley.

The United States in more than one way has been a prominent nation with the idea of predominance and foreseeable Destiny writ large over the dynamic of the nation's 'unison narrative'. The rider is that the United States ought not to be equated with any other pontificating conquistador that has a foreign policy smeared in the rubric of neo-imperialism. American strivings ought not to be clubbed with the exigencies of the other Colonial satraps from Europe, namely, Great Britain, France, Netherlands and Germany in the Asiatic and African spaces.

Manifest Destiny is a palpable argument that separates out the American nation from the rest of the nations, at least in the ideational sense of the term. It's the idea of serendipity or a fortunate occurrence with a well-delineated and engrossingly laid out chance element, which drives the bandwagon of American growth and progression as a nation.

Personages such as Davy Crockett from Tennessee, who was a backwoodsman, were exemplary of the American Dream and the larger idiom of Manifest Destiny. He won the Congress seat thrice in a life time and the idea of giving a speech in a campaign left him exceedingly nervous. Lord helped him as he was able to speak in a lighter vein after all the other speakers had bored the audience stiff with their rote ideological talk.[13] Such tales of frontier man and backwoodsman drawing out the trail in the Oregon pathway with the wagons and the horse's six hooves became the symptomatic idioms of the notion of Manifest Destiny. All these narratives avidly reflect the grandiloquent Manifest Destiny argument that akin to what John Truslow Adams had to contend about the American dream was all about propping up individual skill and entrepreneurship as the common peeve in the American way to rise up in life devoid of a 'Rags to Riches and greedy penchant' normally prevalent in the conceding masses. John Truslow Adams coined the word in his work, *The Epic of America*, where-in he stressed upon the uncharacteristic nature and diffident nature of the individual-centric American dream with the larger good of the nation and the larger society being the other ponderables in the dictum of Manifest Destiny and the grandiloquent American dream.[14] Thus, as a consequence, the indispensability of an American aggrandizement and expanse in the sense of power enhancement and territorial expansion through the purchase of Louisiana and the Missouri compromise, were, too, pinned as the milestones in laying the foundation of the larger expansive manoeuvres of the United States in the far-flung future that happens to be the contemporary context of the post-Trump's Elections America.

'No incident marks the beginning of our trail. With the exception of the Aztecs and the Mayas, no Aboriginal American knew a calendar, and for all of us who lived in the confines of our territory, there was a timeless and dateless quality about time',[15] these sentences have been taken from the Prologue of the historical work, *The Epic of America*, which portrays the dark, dreary and a cliffhanger-like dark brood of the lightning strikes on the crags. This amounts to the large substratum upon which the settlers built their form and civilizational ethos in an alien land, through utilizing all means. It was to be this dark brooding visage of a craggy coast that was to metamorphose into the Hollywood of yore and the advent of the geva-coloured dreams. These idioms served as the base upon which the larger idea of the American interventionism and expansiveness is readily and non-broodingly premised. Onwards the Oregon trail of American interventions and never the usurpations akin to the European firmament!!!!!!!!! Serendipity, it is as part of the larger Oregon Trail!!!!!

John Truslow Adams writes,

> The varied surface of the land was modelled by a giant hand. In the North, a group of great lakes, covering nearly a hundred thousand square miles, held half the fresh water of the entire world. In the great central valley of the Mississippi, drained by a river system four thousand miles long, one could travel in a straight line for four thousand miles, across rolling prairies and sturdy plains.[16]

The alacrity, with which the expanse of territoriality was espoused, as, the key criterion of the founding myth of America, made the American nation strive further for ideational and external pre-eminence with a striving to bring the currency arguments of the grandiloquent America dream into the key parlance of the American nation. Thus, a nation premised upon the Mount Sinai ought to be the Regulator State and amalgamative experience for the larger besieged humanity, also, forms a core corpus of the Manifest Destiny argument in the spirit of the, 'Chosen few'. The Avengers par excellence in the contemporary and unique sense of the term!!!!

The US–Spanish war was a kind of a landmark event and a historical act of American interventionism. The war ushered in the true-blue intent of the US to be more than a moderator for the American sphere. The war was modelled as a first on the MIM instance proffered by President Eisenhower much later in the American narrative. The nation of Spain was the first state to sail across the Atlantic to establish its command over the new world. The Library of Congress Report informs us about the historical and resentful murmurings in Cuba,

> Following the liberation from Spain of mainland Latin America, Cuba was the first to initiate its own struggle for independence. During the years from 1868-1878, Cubans personified by guerrilla fighters known as mambises fought for autonomy from Spain. That war concluded with a treaty that was never enforced. In the 1890's Cubans began to agitate once again for their freedom from Spain. The moral leader of this struggle was José Martí, known as 'El Apóstol', who established the Cuban Revolutionary Party on January 5, 1892 in the United States. Following the *grito de Baire*, the call to arms on February 24, 1895, Martí returned to Cuba and participated in the first weeks of armed struggle when he was killed on May 19, 1895.[17]

The urge for freedom fief and independence was such that the Cubans were not satisfied with the dwindling influence of Spain and wanted to strive for a complete rendition of sovereignty though America, the liberator, later on too created a few conditionality on the sovereignty issue. Keeping in view the perception of the freedom-oriented and oppressed denizens of Cuba, the American succor was much welcome and was never morally illegal and cannot be wiped off the historical slate as a 'crass intervention'.

The Spanish–American war had no serious repercussions on the balance of power situation in Europe as none of the European powers other than Spain became involved in the North American and Cuban project. Robert H Ferrell writes in *American Diplomacy*,

> Likewise as so far as concerned, the two combatants in the war, the war did not permanently impair that good relations. At the Peace Conference, there appeared little enmity between the American and the Spanish delegates. The war gave for the first time, internationally speaking, a vague feeling of fear. Danger and risky adventure and the sentiment of entrepreneurship and reconstruction disappeared in the roar and the aplomb of a national war.[18]

President McKinley during a speech at Atlanta in 1898 affirmed the care of confederate graves to be a national duty. When the President appointed four temporary major generals, he diplomatically chose two confederate generals to commandeer the riposte with the Spaniards.

Ferrell further writes, 'There were many touching evidences of this new national unity, but, perhaps no event was more poignant than the demonstration that occurred, the sixth Massachusetts Regiment marched through Baltimore on its way to encampment'.[19] The Paris Peace Conference happened to be a novae element in the Spanish diplomacy and it is President McKinley who highlighted the various encumbrances of the want of technological advances in the international system that hampered real-time geo-strategic decisions. President McKinley went on to contend, 'When we received the Cable from Admiral Dewey telling of the taking of Philippines, I looked up their location on the Globe. I could not have found out where those darned islands were within 2000 miles'.[20] Newspapers too reported about the want of communications and technology as can be fathomed out, Tis not more than two months since Ya larned whether they islands or canned goods.... Suppose Ya was standing at the corner 4, State Shtreet an' Archey R-Road, wud ya know what car to take to get to the Ph'lipeenees? If yer son pakey were to ask you that where the Philippines islands were, wud you give him any gud idea whether they are in Roshia or just west in the Thracks.[21]

Thus, the distanciation theme in the physical and tangible sense, had to be a grand strategy and an idyllic obfuscation, where-in, the American establishment was finding a way to flout the key driving theme of the American Founding fathers. The key theme was that the American nation would stay away from the entangling alliances of the European ways till the internal girth, power, might and the gargantuan overarch of the American mainland was ordinately established over the larger firmament of the international system.

Richard Olney of Massachusetts, who was also the Attorney General of the American nation during the days of the American war with Spain over Cuba, too, posited the idiom of Manifest Destiny that bore a great semblance with the theme of Monroe Doctrine and the all-flat dominance of the Americans in the Northern continent writ large over the face of the entire sub-continent.[22] Olney went on to lecture in the US Congress,

> The Civilized states of Christendom deal with each other on substantially the same principles that regulate the conduct of the

> individuals. The greater its enlightenment, the more surely every state perceives that its permanent interests require it to be governed by the immutable principles of right and justice. Each, nevertheless, is only to liable to succumb to the temptations offered by be seeming special opportunities for its aggrandizement, and each would rashly imperil its own safety, were it not to remember that for the regard and respect of other states it must be largely dependent upon its own strength and power.[23]

The US Attorney General further contended,

> Today, the United States is practically sovereign on this continent and its fiat is law upon the subjects to which it confirms its interposition. Why? It is not because of pure friendship or goodwill, its simply by reason of its high character as a civilized state, nor because wisdom and justice and equity are the invariable characteristics of the dealings of the United States. It is because, in addition to all other grounds, its infinite resources combined with its isolated position render it master of the situation and practically invulnerable as against any or all other powers.[24]

The battles over Cuba, Philippines and Manila might have been fought away from the American homeland but the fracas and the American adventures were a reflection of and were symptomatic of the idiom of Monroe Doctrine and the striving of grand proportions to keep away the entangling powers from the North American geo-political, geo-economic and geo-strategic scenario. This was undertaken to pass out the time of the American preparation to tackle the world and then finally festoon itself upon the larger firmament of the global system.

Lord Salisbury, too, talks about the Monroe Doctrine and its efficacy in the region under focus. Lord Salisbury went on to contend,

> In the remarks which I have made, I have argued on the theory that the Monroe Doctrine itself is sound. International Law is founded on the general consent of nations, and no statesman, however eminent, and no nation, however powerful, are competent to insert into the coda of international Law, a novel principle which was never recognized before, and which has not been since accepted by the Government of any other country. The United States has a right, like any other nation, to interpose in any controversy by which their own interests are affected, and they are the judge whether those interests are touched and in what measure

> they should be sustained. But, their rights are in no way strengthened or extended by the fact that the controversy affects some territory which is called American.[25]

It can be ferreted out from the media reportage and content analysis of the reports of the time that the US–Spanish war was one of the least talked about war of the 19th century, but it did signify the attainment of power and pelf by the American nation and a kind of stressing on the part of the White House that the American nation had arrived. In the aftermath of the civil war, another significant theme caught the attention of the scholars and the observation of American Politics that a Boundary Commission was passed to be created by the US Congress at the behest of President Cleveland in order to solve the border issues with neighbours and assert the American rights, its people's will in the near neighbourhood as a rising great power of the larger international system.

American diplomacy, its attendant interventionism and the entire American diplomatic tradition are largely European in origin, and hence it is with the Diplomacy of the Old World that the present volume must concern itself with. Europeans have sometimes sought to make their American friends feel as if diplomacy is as American as an Apple pie, and the French Ambassador to the United States, at the turn of the 20th century, Jules Jusserand, once told an American audience that Diplomacy is the art of bringing home the Bacon without spilling the Beans. This may be true, but words, even American words will not remove the European contribution to American Diplomacy. Sir Harold Nicholson, the Diplomat par excellence, has cited several historical and mythological references in his little Book, titled as *Diplomacy*, published on the eve of the second world war. He cites that the art of Diplomacy is old as man; the practice of Diplomacy goes back to the Roman times, where-in the travellers in the nation, were given certificates of travelling consent called as 'Diplomas' by the Roman authorities. Also, the first diplomats were the angels and the Godly messengers who travelled swiftly and were the epitomes of tact, intelligence, oratory and dilligence. Even Sir Ernest Satow has contended, 'Diplomacy is the application of tact and intelligence to the conduct of official relations between the governments of independent states', as mentioned in his work, *A Guide to Diplomatic Practice.*

In the context of the US–Spanish war, Cuba was the precipitating cause of war. Ferrell writes,

> The Ever faithful isle, as it was mentioned in the Spanish Empire, had in mid nineteenth century begun to be embedded by the sentient sentinels of nationalism. Cuban nationalism produced open warfare for a decade beginning in 1868, a long and savage Guerilla conflict between Spanish Military forces and the revolutionaries which was confined largely to the wild and unsettled eastern end to the island and did not afflict the rich and populous western half which includes Havana.[26]

Much before the war cry 'Remember the Maine!' became a stipulated clarion cry and a motoring motif for the Americans. It was posited that America could have entered the war with Spain and attacked Cuba, when, the American warship, much before the sinking of USS Maine, named as Virginius was attacked and its crew were mauled by the Spanish authorities. The talk of the town was that the ship was falsely flying the American flag and the British Ambassador to Cuba attempted a settlement.[27] Thus, what transpired in 1898 with the 'Maine war' could have erupted as a battle in Cuba, much before in 1873.

Thus, it was the idea of Cubans being tormented as suppressed subjects that caused the Americans to intervene in the Cuban badlands, and the expansionist tirade against an American ambition was thus heralded, which was going to be persistent till the America-led Iraq war and many more besieged stations. The US was also involved in discussion with the British Government and Lord Salisbury in the boundary question with Venezuela, where-in, the Americans chose to mediate in the boundary conflict between Great Britain and the Latin American state of Venezuela. Similarly, the American hyphenation of India–Pakistan in its relationship with the American nation has always been resented by India as an affront that unduly internationalizes the Kashmir question, which India considers as being non-negotiable.[28] Thus, the United States of America has to be rather careful that in intervening in far-off conflicts and 'troubles', the national questions of sovereignty and national homeland security concerns, along with the integrity and identity questions, have to be taken into canny consideration. US needs to undertake a balancing act as to how to unearth the roots of its opposition in order to tackle the confrontationists in the longer termish sense to develop and derive a collectivist rationale for the oeuvre of its global and far-flung interventions in the larger international system.

Kenneth Hendrikson writes,

> The 1898 war between the United States and Spain receives relatively little attention in most American history texts, yet it is an event of major importance. The United States emerged as the world's greatest power in the 20th century. In many ways, the war with Spain was a stepping stone from one era of American history to the next, showing Americans that aggressive nationalism could be fraught with danger, even as it was crowned with splendor.[29]

Thus, the defining edge of the double-edged sword of interventions loomed large over the morality statuesque of the American firmament since one of its earliest interventions abiding by its 'sticking to its neighbourhood' policy.

The war in Spain began with a slew of circumstances as none of the nations wanted a warlike or a conflictual situation. Still, one can contend,

> The process began on February 25, 1895 when the revolt against the Cuban rule began in right earnest in Cuba as the revolt was a consequence of a spate of disaffection with the colonial Spanish rule. The Cubans had never been content under Spanish rule and had risen before in 1868-1878 in past occasions without political and military success. One of the involved Cuban leaders was Jose Marti, who had devoted most of his adult life to the cause of independence along with Maximo Gomez and Antonio Maceo. Their rebellious strategy was direct, simple and brutal. They intended to carry out a scorched earth campaign that would make the cost of maintaining control very onerous for the Spaniards. Their goal was independence and from the outset they implied that they would settle for nothing less.[30]

Thus, the American attempt at intervention in Cuba was not much of an extraneous affair, but, a kind of supportive legerdemain and a strategic gamble in tune with its regional one-uppance policy very much in consonance with the Monroe Doctrine and related humanitarianism.

The author further writes, 'In the early stages of military action, the Americans set up a military junta and a rule of the rebels in order to counter the Spanish machismo. This place was established in New York city with the aim and the avowed objective to carry on and sustain propaganda activities for the Cuban cause in the land and amidst the hoi polloi of the United States'.[31] It was believed that in the cause of the economic and strategic reasons, the American establishment would intervene as the entire notion of the morality tide of humanitarianism, was, too involved as the rationale behind a future American intervention. Thus, keeping in view the issue of cold war confrontation and the Cuban Missile crisis of the decade of the sixties, the Americans were with the Cubans for once. Also, the American zeal for 'exceptional interventionism' was buttressed surprisingly as early as in the 19th century, by the Cuban rebels themselves. Thus, the xenophobia and the air and palaver of fashionable distrust of a nation that intends to regulate the conflict centres with its near-to-gargantuan superstrength is rather uncalled for and is rather unfathomable for a purveyor of realist and idealist Real Politique, all rolled into one skill set for the larger humanity and its attendant humanitarian concerns.

The Spaniards were not in the pink of their military health and were not well prepared for the war as they were expecting a diplomatic solution for the fracas with Washington.[32] Even Senator Henry M. Teller proclaimed before the war that the United States did not have much of a military interest in the situation brewing in Cuba.[33] Thus, the Americans were not interested in the going-ons in Cuba with a wayward intention to meddle and be meddlesome with known and unknown intent.

Even the American military forces were not well prepared for the war, as, in the entire gamut of American military numbering around 114,000, was, scattered all across the length and breadth of the nation. One internal American debate was that in the case of the war with Spain, the brunt of the war would be undertaken by the Navy and at best the Army would be only deployed in a secondary and a supportive role. Also, the various Americans were not confident about the efficacy of a war with Spain.[34] The Havana Governor after hearing about the might of the Americans advancing about in steamers, despite initial chaos during the march on, could not be convinced initially to the idea of surrendering before the advancing American forces. Another question that engaged the attention of General Sagasta in Havana was how could the surrendered Spanish Army be allowed to retain their weapons after the surrender had taken place. Also, before the final surrender, Captain Arthur H. Lee from the American navy got the message conveyed to the General Toral of Havana that if the Spaniards surrendered quickly, then, the American Navy would not be engaged and the American projectiles would not rain in on the city of Havana.

The Spanish General Toral refused to surrender that made the American Navy frigates fire cannons on the City and a large number of ammunition projectiles landed in the besieged city. Still, after the damage was being taken care of after the Spanish surrender, the Americans figured out that not much material and collateral damage had come the way of the city of Havana. General Shafter was a very cunning practitioner of the trade of chicanery-infused diplomacy, where-in the Americans told General Toral that after the Spanish surrender, no harm would come to the Spanish soldiers and also the armaments would be returned to the soldiers. Even, the soldiers would be set free to rejoin the Spanish establishment.[35] But, General Toral reminded them that he needed an opportunity to communicate with the motherland in order to convey to the Spanish mainland that he was surrendering. Thus, the entire military circus went ahead after the Americans managed a surrender in Cuba and the wishes of Cuban freedom and alacrity came true. Thus, in whichever way, the grandiloquent American military and flexing motorcade and the Uncle Sam escapades were initiated in a sedate, sterile and a far-seated war in Cuba, which was to turn into another station and staging post of the cold war in the next century to come with palpable ramifications for the mandarins of American foreign policy and the novae outward-looking externalities of US foreign policy in line with the quintessential Monroe Doctrine thought of the day. Let's delve deeper into the fundamentals of the Monroe Doctrine.

Jay Sexton writes in the work, *The Monroe Doctrine*,

> President James Monroe's 1823 message to Congress declaring opposition to European colonization in the Western Hemisphere became the cornerstone of nineteenth-century American statecraft. The Monroe Doctrine proclaimed anti-colonial principles, yet it rapidly became the myth and means for subsequent generations of politicians to pursue expansionist foreign policies. The crucial episodes in nineteenth and early-twentieth-century foreign relations¯westward expansion in the 1840s, Civil War diplomacy, the imperialism of 1898, entrance into World War I, and the establishment of the League of nations, were framed by the Doctrine as its meaning evolved to suit the dreams and fears of an American empire.[36]

The author further enlightens the audience,

> President James Monroe laid the foundation of American foreign policy when he said, 'The American continents ... are henceforth not to be considered as subjects for colonization by any European powers'.

> Originating as a principle of non-intervention in the newly independent countries of Latin America, the Monroe Doctrine was eventually invoked for American interventions, a metamorphosis that occurred during the nineteenth century and here attracts Sexton's examination. He ties changes in the doctrine's application to several factors: antagonistic U.S.-UK relations, U.S. continental expansion, and U.S. imperial acquisitions in the late 1890s. Narrating specific diplomatic situations, as in Oregon and Mexico, Sexton underscores American leaders' perception of foreign threat up to the 1860s, which materialized during the Civil War when the British indicated they might recognize the Confederacy. The dissipation of disunion anxieties after 1865 cleared the way for reinterpretation of the doctrine by the Roosevelt Corollary, by which TR justified his actions in Panama.[37]

It was to be generally perceived that the American newfound girth's mirth could not be equated with the idea of Colonialism and Imperialism but a roundly American genre of expansionism dutifully became the order of the day for the American nation and its subsequent foreign policy. The rising comparison with the British army and naval might and its attendant and all-pervading Colonial might and expanse was one of the significant reasons that led to the idea of all important metamorphosis in the American foreign policy thought and implication. With the advent of a will to sustain and excel externally, in the Atlantic moat, the Americans relegated to the backburner, the American paradigm of staying away from the 'entangling alliances of the Continental Europe' and marched on to a newfound land of superior pelf, power and power strides. America was to be reinvented and it was here to stay, but, with a delimitation of the Colonial streak of the continental Europe. Thus, the American expanse was to ride roughshod over other nationalities, trade outposts and principalities, but, with its own version and genre of expansionism and an adroit foreign policy paradigm with the added hue of philanthropy and welfarist verve.

The fear that drove the issuing of Monroe's message was that the Holy Alliance (France, Austria, Russia and Prussia) would use their Troppau Circular of 1820 to justify interfering on the side of Spain to crush the independence movements in South America. The American fear was that we would end up surrounded by some combination of the Holy Alliance, Spain and Britain. Also, the American transformation of its adroit interference flavour of a policy links itself up with the fear reflected in the American Federalist papers.

The American federalist papers presented quite vociferously the idiom of the fear and the threat of the external foe and the internal antagonists that made the Americans look ahead and alter their inward looking arc of foreign policy. With the European powers and with their naval might, trade dispensations and their imperial overarch, breathing down the neck of an already beleaguered South America, the Americans had to invent a non-vivant qualifier approach. This approach amounted to the idiom of counteracting the amphibious colonial intent of the European powers such as France, Austria, Russia and Prussia. Thus, the American policymakers had to invent a new conciliatory as well as an aggressive mould of policy that could at least keep a deft watch upon the shenanigans of the European Continentalists. The message had to be that America' backyard had to be guarded through selfsame resources and by a power amplificatory foreign policy in the Atlantic moat.

Grace Livingstone in the America's backyard has attempted a striving to annihilate the America's bugbears in South America. The author contends,

> 'Using newly-declassified documents, Grace Livingstone reveals the U.S. role in the darkest periods of Latin American history including Pinochet's coup in Chile, the Contra War in Nicaragua and the death squads in El Salvador. She shows how the U.S. administration used the War on Terror as a new pretext for intervention and how it tried to destabilize leftwing governments and push back the 'pink tide' washing across the Americas. America's Backyard also has chapters on drugs, economy and culture. It explains why U.S. drug policy has caused widespread environmental damage, yet failed to reduce the supply of cocaine and looks at the U.S. economic stake in Latin America and the strategies of the big corporations. Today Latin Americans are demanding respect and an end to the Washington Consensus. Will the White House listen?[38] Still, intervention in Latin America was a necessity.

The American tirade of what was initiated in Cuba in the Spanish-American war, found, a new challenge in the form of the left dictatorships and regimes as they managed to come to power in some of the South American nations and in the larger region. In a way, the Americans had to intervene in nations such as Nicaragua and El Salvador out of the necessity of containing the Soviet and the crassly communist dominoes that were impacting the American homeland right in the superpower's backyard.

The American Federalist papers too can be delved inside with some detail if the content of Foreign policy segments needs to be unearthed in a more incisive manner in the US mainland. Competition and trade equations with nations such as Britain and France were recorded as the reasons why the Americans too needed not to eulogize war but cooperation. Still, keeping in view the all-pervading influence of the European Colonists, the Americans had to select a slightly and partially war-mongering and expansionist intent in order to live true to the humanist intent as well as the ides of a war-thronging technics. All in all, the idiom of national interest reigns supreme with all probable permutations and combinations. One can delve inside the dynamics of the content of the Federalist Paper No. 4 in the context of the question of war and foreign policy. The Federalist Paper No. 4 runs,

> Tis too true, however disgraceful it may be to human nature, that nations in general will make war whenever they have a prospect of getting anything by it; nay, absolute monarchs will often make war when their nations are to get nothing by it, but for the purposes and objects merely personal, such as thirst for military glory, revenge for personal affronts, ambition, or private compacts to aggrandize or support their particular families or partisans. These and a variety of other motives, which affect only the mind of the sovereign, often lead him to engage in wars not sanctified by justice or the voice and interests of his people. But, independent of these inducements to war, which are more prevalent in absolute monarchies, but which well deserve our attention, there are others which affect nations as often as kings; and some of them will on examination be found to grow out of our relative situation and circumstances.[39]

The Federalist Paper further informs us, 'With France and with Britain we are rivals in the fisheries, and can supply their markets cheaper than they can themselves, notwithstanding any efforts to prevent it by bounties on their own or duties on foreign fish'.[40] Thus, apart from the context of high seas, the question of trade contentions and trade tussles with the bigwigs in the European continents also led to the idea of competition with the Old World, and the novae overarch chose to call it a day for the European traditionalist powers with their colonial and imperial objectives and aims.

The Federalist papers also aimed at tackling the naval and the material might of individual nations such as Great Britain and urged the founding fathers to showcase a novae policy paradigm for the Americans in order to excel pragmatically in world fraught with new trade and expansionist challenges.

The context of the Federalist papers too highlights the same rationale in the context of Great Britain and other nations. The Federalist Paper No. 4 contends,

> We have heard much of the fleets of Britain, and the time may come, if we are wise, when the fleets of America may engage attention. But if one national government, had not so regulated the navigation of Britain as to make it a nursery for seamen—if one national government had not called forth all the national means and materials for forming fleets, their prowess and their thunder would never have been celebrated. Let England have its navigation and fleet—let Scotland have its navigation and fleet—let Wales have its navigation and fleet—let Ireland have its navigation and fleet—let those four of the constituent parts of the British empire be under four independent governments, and it is easy to perceive how soon they would each dwindle into comparative insignificance.

The Federalist papers too refer to the question of internal security, stability, stolidity, unity and integrity of the nation.

The content expressed is,

> Apply these facts to our own case. Leave America divided into thirteen or, if you please, into three or four independent governments—what armies could they raise and pay—what fleets could they ever hope to have? If one was attacked, would the others fly to its succor, and spend their blood and money in its defense? Would there be no danger of their being flattered into neutrality by its specious promises, or seduced by a too great fondness for peace to decline hazarding their tranquillity and present safety for the sake of neighbors, of whom perhaps they have been jealous, and whose importance they are content to see diminished?

Thus, the questions of the internal stolidity and the rapacious perch of the external foes, as endangering the internal girth of the American homeland, were always posited as the questions and quests to be grappled with. This can very easily be comprehended and equated with as the grandiloquent founding myth and the lore of the American nation and its attendant *vox populi*.

The content and the legerdemain of the Federalist papers echoes a concern as to the state of internal security in the nation and to the destabilizing challenges and influences of the external foes in the form of nations such as France and Britain and other able-bodied European continentalists. The law of the land and the larger international system had still to be adhered to and adroitly followed. The following chapter delves inside the historical and legal perspectives of International Law that play a key role apart from academic debates into the practical working of the global comity of nations with the pertinent quest for the answer to an American Question: How can the American Interventionism, as it is perceived by a cabal of anti-liberal nations and academia, be rationalized and a constructive and optimistic thesis be created which that the American interventions in the kosher legal, political and moral light.

NOTES

1. 'Yellow Journalism: Willaim Randolph Hearst'. http://www.pbs.org/crucible/bio_hearst.html. Accessed 10 April 2017.
2. Ibid.
3. 'Spanish American War'. http://www.history.com/topics/spanish-american-war. Accessed 10 April 2018.
4. Ibid.
5. Calude, Inis L., Jr, *Swords Into Ploughshares: The Problems and Progress of International Organizations*, New York: Random House, 1998, pp. 10–30.
6. Ibid.
7. Musicant, Evan, *Empire By Default: The Spanish American War and the Dawn of the American Century*, New York: Henry Holt, 1998.
8. Ibid.
9. White, Trumball, 'Our War With Spain For Cuba's Freedom', HC Hudgins, 1898.
10. Ibid.
11. Trask, D., 'The Spanish American War', https://www.loc.gov/rr/hispanic/1898/trask.html. Accessed 10 April 2017.
12. Ibid.
13. 'Manifest Destiny'. http://www.glencoe.com/sec/socialstudies/ose/tar05_nat/docs/chap12.pdf. Accessed 19 March 2017.
14. Adams, John T., *The Epic of America*, New York: Simon Publications, 2001, pp. 1–15.
15. Ibid., p. 3.
16. Ibid., pp. 4–6.
17. Library of Congress Document, United States, 'The World of 1898: The Spanish-American War'. https://www.loc.gov/rr/hispanic/1898/intro.html. Accessed 1 March 2018.
18. Ferrell, Robert H., *American Diplomacy*, New York: WW Norton, 1959, pp. 360–370.
19. Ibid., p. 370.
20. Ibid. p. 362.
21. Ibid. p. 363.
22. Richard Olney, US Attorney General, US Congress Lecture, 1897.
23. Ibid.
24. Ibid.
25. Buck, Paul H.,'The Road to Reunion: 1865-1900', Boston, 1937.
26. Calcott, Wilfred Harvey, 'The Caribbean Policy of the United States: 1890-1920', Columbia University Press, 1971.

27. Feidel, Frank, 'Dissent in Three American Wars'. Cambridge, Massachusetts, 1970.
28. *The Indian Express*, "India raises concern over Trumps' Mediation", April 2017.
29. Hendrikson, Kenneth, *The Spanish American War*, New York: Greenwood Publishing House, 2003.
30. Ibid., p. 17.
31. Ibid., pp. 18–20.
32. Congressional Record, 55th Congress, 2nd session, 17 March 1898, pp. 2916–19.
33. Ibid.
34. Ibid.
35. Hendrikson, op. cit. p. 37.
36. Sexton, Jay, 'The Monroe Doctrine: Empire and Nation in Nineteenth Century America', Hill and Wang, 2012.
37. Ibid.
38. Livingstone, Grace, *America's Backyard: The United States and Latin America from the Monroe Doctrine to the War on Terror*, London, UK: Zed Books, 2009.
39. Yale Law Scholl, Lilian Goldman Law Library, 'The Federalist Papers No. 4'. Documents in Law, History and Diplomacy.
40. Ibid.

3

The International Law Perspective on Pre-emptive War and Humanitarian Intervention: An Objective Dekko

I might initiate the deliberations with the statement that it's a rather dubious claim by the left and the attendant commies that United States of America has committed acts of genocidal proportions in nearly all its humanitarian interventions. To them, the dictatorships par excellence of the order of Saddam Hussein and Kim Jong Il and Kim Jong Un are the barometers of the larger world's resistance to the staid high-handedness and vitriol heaped upon an unsuspecting world by a hegemonic cacophony about its morality, United States of America. The question that might engage a reader is that why the criticism and pejorative narratives about America appear first in the narrative when the author intends to defend the much maligned narrative of American humanitarian interventions.

This anti-American pogrom has done wonders for the larger European University people and a few avant-garde places in South America and South Asia. The author's answer to the lopsided criticism being accorded the first place is that the cantankerous cacophony of the lopsided and vituperative shibboleths of attacks on the United States have been so rampant that they make themselves hilariously loud and engaging with being all over the floor of academia. This factoid makes the tormented and besieged author give a due ranting place to the commie narrative even in his partisan narrative on American interventions.

The narrative of humanitarian interventions has been hijacked by the left and commie snippets and rationalizations on castigating and ridiculing the American status as a Regulator and monitor nation state. Thus, the misinterpretations by the left and the commies follow in the context of article 51 of the UN charter and its various subsets; the dark spawned gerrymandering then brings in the stipulations of the Article 7 of the UN charter, where-in the dystopia of 'reverend' and so-called activist-expose-intelligence takes over in the stout and dark gargoyles and serpentine labyrinths of left, and commie filibustering in the academia. Akin to other political, diplomatic and strategic spheres, the notion of pre-emptive warfare is a much bandied term that serially lambasts the American intrusions in the larger third world.

One can use the Eagle vision of the pre-emptive warfare that has been the quintessential stratagem of the United States, where-in, the nation garners the collective spirit and the military–economic might of the homeland in order to forecast and prognosticate about a foe who is about to engage in an misadventure. The rabid misadventure might be on the homeland through a September 11 catastrophe–like ministration or a punitive attack on a near or a far-off ally or a member of the larger American coalition.

The notion of pre-emptive war has been deftly championed by the personages such as President Bush, Jr. The CFR writes that pre-emptive war is a kind of attrition waged by the United States that was never a trademark essence of the US policy, but now it has become one of the cornerstones of the US retaliatory paradigm globally. The CFR writes,

> Until the end of the 19th century, the United States was generally reluctant to use military force abroad, with limited exceptions, to defend American interests and expand the national territory. During the 20th century, the U.S. became a great power, and conducted many military interventions around the world. Nevertheless, U.S. policymakers have generally stated a preference to use force only as a last resort.[1]

Then, one can delve inside why the American avant-garde strategists reneged and attempted a new coalition with the idiom of pre-emptive warfare. There is not much of a difference between pre-emptive war and preventive warfare. This idiom can be sustained by delving inside the notion as advanced by the CFR release. The CFR release informs us,

> The difference between preemptive war and preventive war is not a matter of semantics. Rather, it is a matter of timing that has implications

> for whether an act is justified or not. Traditionally, preemption constitutes a 'war of necessity' based on credible evidence of imminent attack against which action is justified under international law as enshrined in the self-defense clause (Article 51) of the UN Charter.[2]

But, the Bush administration had expanded the definition to include actions that more closely resemble preventive war. The CFR reports, Preventive wars are essentially 'wars of choice' that derive mostly from a calculus of power, rather than the precedent of international law, conventions and practices. In choosing preventive wars, policymakers project that waging a war, even if unprovoked, against a rising adversary sooner is preferable to an inevitable war later when the balance of power no longer rests in their favor.[3]

The rabid left and commie community that raises a voice against the notion of preventive war is that a forecasted and prognosticated war based on flimsy or no evidence before the World Body, United Nations, is an American misdemeanour and superior profligacy.

The pejorative idea is that no pre-emptive war can be undertaken in the name of protecting the American population. The practical question that can be pertinently raised is that how can the striving of any democratic and liberal nation be curtailed and purloined in the name of a nebulous higher morality. Also, as an attendant fact how can the American homeland be asked to wait for a second September 11 to occur and why can't the American nation and its establishment have the sovereign rights to protect its nationality in the name of a legitimate R2P, that is, the Right to Protect. Thus, the American profligacy is bandied about as a criminal act under the ambit of the humanitarian law façade, while the ***communist internationale*** promptly snatches away the right to protect from the nimble Americans in the context of its own homeland and sovereign rights. Why commit this perfidy on the always on the roll but besieged America? The entire American nation can forge a 'Rally around the Flag phenomenon' when the insidious intent of the foe is rather clear to the entire world and to the cocksure American intelligence establishment. The larger idea being that Americans have the inalienable right to secure their liberty, happiness, property and well being going by the context of the hallowed Declaration of Independence as they are an apt essay in vile victimhood.[4]

The idiom and practice of Intelligence plays a significant role in the larger quest to find a suitable landing ground for the question of pre-emptive war.

Richard Beets elucidates on the general and larger idiom as we are technically taking up broader themes and issues. Richard Betts informs us,

> Intelligence plays very different roles depending on whether the context is preemptive war or preventive war. To justify preemptive war both to the international community and to the American people, the U.S. must have solid evidence that not only does a state have the means of attack, but also the intention to do so *imminently*. According to Richard Betts, obtaining clarity about intent is often difficult. The picture is often murky because of conflicting state signals, inadequate insight into the inner workings of enemies' top leadership, or imperfect understandings of the goals and methods of terrorist organizations.[5]

He further writes,

> Military maneuvers along a contested border can constitute a readiness drill as easily as the buildup to a first wave of attack. Sophisticated sensors that track troop and weaponry movements are limited by the effects of camouflage or subterfuge. At home, the U.S. still has poor insight into the operations of terrorist cells despite the creation of the Department of Homeland Security and enactment of the USA Patriot Act. The espionage network remains thin in critical areas of the world where anti-Americanism runs deep.[6]

Thus, whatever resources can the American establishment garner for its intelligence gathering, the American strivings need to be redoubled with more precision if the clean-up act and the war on terror have to be initiated with the theme of completion and a quantum of success globally and in the American homeland. The American intervention in post-Pulwama scenario is an apt reminder of the regulator role.

International cooperation and the role played by the international organizations have been found wanting, for instance, in the American Pre-emptive effort in the state of Iraq after the military victory over Saddam Hussein. The Congressional Budget Office informs that the American stay potential in Iraq has been hobbled by financial constraints too as the other nationalities in the 'Coalition of the Willing' have been found wanting in donating much critical moolah. The Congressional Budget Office writes,

> The Bush administration implicitly believes this turn away from multilateralism will either not harm or will in fact advance American interests. The post-conflict situation in Iraq leads to a different

> conclusion. Without significant numbers of international troops to help, roughly one-half of the deployable U.S. Army, or 180,000 of 300,000 active personnel, is now tasked to Iraq. However, the Congressional Budget Office estimates that in steady-state, the Army can support a deployment of only 3 to 5 2/3 brigades without withdrawing from other global commitments.[7]

If this situation lasts for much longer, Michael O'Hanlon warns that the US Army will 'break'.[8] The pace and scope of Iraq's economic recovery has been hobbled by the lack of participation by international non-governmental organizations. Still, the NSS or the National Security Strategy of the United States made an effort in 2002 to concretize a case for Pre-emptive and Preventive war, where-in, the American nation can forge a case for pre-filling the preparatory gaps for saving its entrepreneurial and deftly inclined denizens. The American establishment can pooh-pooh the criticality of the European continentals and the other observant folks in the fashionable arcades of academia, as, the R2P idiom is part of any normal nation state's security construct. Thus, the American rationale for the larger world and the troubled spots is that a powerful nation of the order of the United States of America ought to serve as the International balancer or the Regulator-monitor country. As the nations quarrel over petty egoistic and major matters, then, the various nations can go ahead and be on the necessary look-out for a fair leader such as Washington to circumscribe the comity of states as few nations do not seem to fall in line.

If we were to have a strategic look at the idea of pre-emptive war, then how can one comprehend President Trump's decision to up-the-ante on North Korea in May 2017. President Trump as a candidate had declared for a decision and a choice against the idiom of Pre-emptive war as the outward outreach of Washington was supposed to be withdrawn, but in the light of the Asian call to let the Americans be the arbiter of their security, new signposts have been achieved. The withdrawal of the American juggernaut has not exactly happened, but instead the American establishment is going ahead with its responses to Syria and the Korean question with an imminent strike against the North Korean dictatorship. Though the 2018 detente premised upon a nuclear hand shake removes the bland necessity of conflict between America, its allies and the Korean state and China. Thus, the R2P response is very much here, which entails a renewed and revitalized move to oust the North Korean dictator, Kim Jong Un and his communist junta in Pyongyang. What might dilly dally the American military response to North Korean nuclear tests, is, the possibility of initiating a catastrophic confrontation with China leading to the destruction of Asian capitals of the order of Seoul and Tokyo in the near neighbourhood of Kim Jong Un's communist junta. North Korea has lambasted the aggressive streak of the United States with the North Korean establishment presenting a strong face to the American power insistence, which does not amount to bland power throwing and the attendant posturing.

Chris Perez reports in the *New York Post*,

> If the US comes with reckless military maneuvers, then we will confront it with the [North Korea's] pre-emptive strike. Han also blasted President Trump for 'making trouble' with his 'aggressive' tweets and said the North Korean military will conduct their nuclear tests whenever they like. We've got a powerful nuclear deterrent already in our hands, and we certainly will not keep our arms crossed in the face of a US preemptive strike.[9]

Thus, Perez further reports,

> The strike would likely include both missiles and bombs, while also using of cyber and special operations on the ground. The US intelligence officials told the outlet that even plans for such an assault could cause the already on-edge communist nation—which has so far conducted five nuclear weapons tests—to launch its own attack on South Korea or US ships in the region. The leadership in North Korea has shown absolutely no sign or interest in diplomacy or dialogue with any of the countries involved in this issue.[10]

North Korea has expressed no fear of the American might and has promised a thermonuclear response in the face of American strikes on its homeland. Nika Knights writes in *Common Dreams*,

> In an exclusive interview with the *Associated Press*, Vice Minister Han Song Ryol said that 'Pyongyang has determined the Trump administration is "more vicious and more aggressive" than that of his predecessor, Barack Obama', *AP* writes. He added that North Korea will keep building up its nuclear arsenal in 'quality and quantity' and said Pyongyang is ready to go to war if that's what Trump wants.[11]

Nika Knight further reports,

> In a statement attributed to the North Korean Foreign Ministry's Institute for Disarmament and Peace, officials also warned that the

> U.S. introduces into the Korean peninsula, the world's biggest hotspot, huge nuclear strategic assets, seriously threatening peace and security of the peninsula and pushing the situation there to the brink of a war. This has created a dangerous situation in which a thermonuclear war may break out any moment.[12]

Thus, the zealous American instinct in the context of Pyongyang too happens to be a gamble and a risk that is meant to be underwritten by South Korea and the Nippon (Japan). The years of conflict can transform into another edition of the Korean war of the 50s and thus a deft balancing act is required in the Peninsular region. All these brouhaha about the Korean R2P act is too linked with the American over-lordship and role as a regulator in the tarred terrain in Korea. Still, with the failure of talks in Hanoi, Vietnam, the onus lies with President Trump to bring back North Korea back on a negotiating table.

NOTES

1. Council For Foreign Affairs, 'The Bush Administration's Doctrine of Preemption: How When and Where?', http://www.cfr.org/world/bush-administrations-doctrine-preemption-prevention-/p6799. Accessed 1 May 2018.
2. Ibid.
3. Ibid.
4. The American Declaration of Independence, USGPTO.
5. Betts, Richard K., 'Striking First: A History of Thankfully Lost Opportunities'. *Ethics and International Affairs,* 17(1).
6. Ibid.
7. Congressional Budget Office, 'Letter to the Honorable Robert Byrd regarding the U.S. military's ability to sustain an occupation in Iraq'. http://www.cbo.gov/showdoc.cfm?index=4515& sequence=0., Accessed on 1 May 2017..
8. O'Hanlon, Michael, 'Breaking the Army'. *The Washington Post,* 3 July 2003.
9. Perez, Chris, 'North Korea Blasts Aggressive Trump Amid Reports of Preemptive Strike', *The New York Post,* 13 April 2017.
10. Ibid.
11. Knights, Nika, 'North Korea Warns of Thermonuclear War After Trump Threatens Strike'. https://www.commondreams.org/news/2017/04/14/north-korea-warns-thermonuclear-war-after-trump-threatens-strike. Accessed 3 May 2017.
12. Ibid.

4

The Bells of the Armageddon: The Contours of Conflict in North Korea

APART from a strictly legalese-oriented dimension to the Korean conflict, a quaint but clearly defined political dimension is too part of the larger debate on Preemptive war, in the thought trail of smelling a foe and his ministrations: 'There's a fire and an inferno of capitalist swill burning outside with the outliers. So let's all sit inside the cave and rejoice the clarion call of the commander, the Regulator and let's celebrate and mourn collectively in a civilized mass like good and moral people do and never go out in see the blaze with the outliers'. That is how the quintessential Communist plight amounts to as the collectivization of the hoi polloi takes precedence over innovation, development and the cause célèbre of freedom of opinion and dissent. Thus, the North Korean troubles too brew up in the same manner, where-in the entire nation led by the dictator par excellence in Pyongyang is being lambasted upon. President Trump has declared, 'A major, major conflict with North Korea is possible. We would love to solve things diplomatically but it is very difficult', as reported in most of the national dailies in India. It has been reported in *Reuters*,

> He also said he wants South Korea to pay the cost of the U.S. THAAD anti-missile defense system, which he estimated at $1 billion, and intends to renegotiate or terminate a U.S. free trade pact with South Korea because of a deep trade deficit with Seoul. Trump said North Korea was his biggest global challenge. He lavished praise on Chinese President Xi Jinping for Chinese assistance in trying to rein in Pyongyang. The two leaders met in Florida earlier this month.

The United States is also attempting to outdo the histrionics of President Kim Jong Un akin to his Father, 'Il' as Washington intends to slap sanctions on Pyongyang in order to tame the dragonlet with the support of the Chinese Premier. The entire scare scenario is akin to the era of Ping-Pong Diplomacy, where-in the Americans led by Secretary of State, Henry Kissinger, succeeded in making friends with the Chinese Premier, Mao in a master stratagem to sequester the Soviet Union in the year 1971 as part of the policy of containment of Soviet Union. That clandestine summit had a far-reaching impact upon the entire BoP game in the then *au courant* international system.

The entire amalgam of the Cold War is getting a pride of place now. The nation of North Korea was built over the Korean war when the forces of Douglas McArthur faced the Chinese hordes near the vicinity of the 38th parallel all the way up to the precincts of the Yalu river. The mass casualties nearly turned the Korean peninsula into a kind of hellish inferno for the Americans and the Chinese alike. These developments out of the history set-piece remind us of the turbulent past and the vitriol of a war-torn Korean peninsula, which led to the gruesome partition tale of the North and South Korea. But with, 'Xi trying very hard', in the Korean quagmire, as President Trump calls the entire Chinese Diplomatic striving, there are still opportunities left for this explosive segment of the Asiatic space. Since the North Korean entry into a treaty-making exercise with the 'rest', they have mercilessly flouted their international law understanding with nations such as Japan and South Korea. The deal in the 1990s of accepting the global 'norm setting' in lieu of the supplies of Food grains, from the United States of America too has not augured well for the 'troubled region' of the world.

The nuclear device tests and the ballistic missile tests undertaken by the North Korean autarch, Kim Jong Un have led to the idiom of growing and palpable diplomatic tensions in the Korean and the larger regional firmament. President Trump's tweet says it all about the American opprobrium and anger, 'North Korea disrespected the wishes of China and its highly respected President when it launched, though unsuccessfully, a missile today. Bad'! Thus, the Good and the Bad, the 'Us and the them', paradigm is making the rounds in the regional firmament, where-in the question remains whether the Chinese fit in the appellation of being the 'Ugly' part of the paradigm, though they are the designated interlocutors now in the regional fracas, and according to President Trump, the Regime has 'disrespected China'.

The cold war–era teleserial MASH nicely portrayed the vicissitudes of war and conflict in any region of the larger international system. The mayhem caused by the conflict with the attendant larger human misery gets a sardonic reflection in the crazy narrative of the war in Korea where-in MASH is a crack Medical Unit posted in Korea during the times of the gory Korean war. A full blow-out conflict is not what any Statesman would hanker after but when personages such as Kim Jong Un militate against the international comprehension of pelf, piety and order, then cudgels of cleansing have to be taken up. Also, the repeated stories of the closed socio-political set-up in Pyongyang with the dull and drab brown robes and the smell of kettle and wood in a shack still stymie the North Korean bandwagon that is miles in the backyard of its open South Korean brother.

There is an entire chronology of the Nuclear and Missile technology between North Korea and the United States. The Arms Control Association Factsheet promptly informs us, 'In 1994, faced with North Korea's announced intent to withdraw from the nuclear Nonproliferation Treaty (NPT), which requires non-nuclear weapon states to forswear the development and acquisition of nuclear weapons, the United States and North Korea signed the Agreed Framework. Under this agreement, Pyongyang committed to freezing its illicit plutonium weapons program in exchange for aid'. Later on in the pantheon of the six-party talks carried on between North Korea and the Western nations, the North Korean ruling dispensation vowed to abandon developing nuclear weapons and the attendant nuclear programmes. It was since the year 2009 that the North Koreans have emerged as the nuke-wise, recalcitrant nation state that has not agreed to eschew its nuclear ambitions and designs in the larger vortex of global diplomacy. The United States too has been asked this poser many a times that when Iraq and Saddam Hussein crossed the boundaries of civilization, then they earned a full-fledged coalition of the willing, which was heaped upon them by the corrective Pentagon. But when Pyongyang recalibrates its policy every three months and cocks a snook at the US every now and then, the threshold is taken to the next keel. Thus, the pertinent poser in the larger regional context is that how long can the nuclear conflagration can be avoided and how many more 'unsuccessful tests' are in the waiting before President Trump attempts 'a regional rejig' or something more than that as the American Secretary of State, Rex Tillerson, has defiantly declared in the lurking shadows of the USS Carl Vinson that the spate of 'unsuccessful tests' in the Korean Peninsula will lead to 'catastrophic consequences'. The vulnerability of Tokyo, Seoul and the trans-Pacific American homeland calls for confronting the persistent nuclear blackmail by the North Korea's rapacious Dictator, which is more than an exercise in personal psychological study.

Apart from the case study of North Korea, the interventionist zeal of the United States has been often tempered by the practicalities of security, annihilation through Nukes and the attendant BoP conventions and convictions in the affected region and the concerned nation state. In a manner, the American role playing in lands that are far away from its homeland needs to be comprehended through a different lens. The American power and its 'allied strength', spread across the seven seas and the continents, needs to be realized as a boon to the entire international system, where-in the accidental and largely coincidental stature of the United States as a leader nation is crucial for the upkeep of global order in the light of nation-centric, region-centric imbalances and profligacies.

5

The International Law Perspective: A Delving-Inside Exercise

GOING by and adhering to the norms of Public International Law, preventive conflict management is a specific sphere of study. Prevention of conflict can be ascertained through the stipulations provided in the UN Charter through Article 51 and its myriad sub-provisions. Chapter VII conditionalities of observing and monitoring mutations in the international order along with sanctioning economically and militarily the recalcitrant nations is a mainframe contention in the context of preventive detention of countries and their selfish and self-seeking motives ordained by their respective national interests.

UN Charter's Article 51 has the following stipulations:

> Nothing in the present Charter shall impair the inherent right of individual or collective self-defence, if, an armed attack occurs against a Member of the United Nations, until the Security Council has taken measures necessary to maintain international peace and security. Measures taken by Members in the exercise of this right of self-defence shall be immediately reported to the Security Council and shall not in any way affect the authority and responsibility of the Security Council under the present Charter to take at any time such action, as, it deems necessary in order to maintain or restore international peace and security.[1]

Thus, the stipulations of the UN Chapter VII impart the right to self-defence in the frame of maintaining and sustaining order in the context of America.

The art of pre-emption has been mentioned and described with ubiquitous aplomb, where-in, the nations, leaders and armies have been known to presage and forecast an antagonist intent and design and take ameliorative measures. The right conferred through the Montevideo Convention too places the bonus of sovereignty upon nations such as the United States. Thus, prognosticating a conflict scenario, is, also now a part of scenario building in the art of war and peace practiced by myriad nations. It is clearly mentioned that the member nations can adhere to the idiom of preventive air action initially, in, the light of the activities of the Military Staff Committee that works in tandem with the UN Security Council (UNSC). Thus, the idiom of pre-emptive action premised upon the ideal of Collective Security has never been a non-reality and a strict no-no instrument of peace as is often propagandistically asserted by the left and communist critiques of the notion of the 'liberal war doctrine'. The same can be pinpointed as documental assertions in the light of the liberal doctrine of pre-emption as the medical and the international Peacenik's doctor's notion of prevention is better than cure is always a sine qua non in individual and stately capacities. The relevant articles in this connection happen to be Articles 44 and 45, which can be read as follows:

Article 44

When the Security Council has decided to use force it shall, before calling upon a Member not represented on it to provide armed forces in fulfilment of the obligations assumed under Article 43, invite that Member, if the Member so desires, to participate in the decisions of the Security Council concerning the employment of contingents of that Member's armed forces.[2]

Article 45

In order to enable the United Nations to take urgent military measures, Members shall hold immediately available national air-force contingents for combined international enforcement action. The strength and degree of readiness of these contingents and plans for their combined action shall be determined within the limits laid down in the special agreement or agreements referred to in Article 43, by the Security Council with the assistance of the Military Staff Committee.[3]

Thus, the ideal of collectivized and national interest–oriented preventive war has been duly enshrined in the UN norm setting, and to refer to the leadership provided by nations such as the United States in building UN-ordained Coalitional sinks for global security is a matter of grave concern. The critiques deliberately misread the statutes of International Law and the United Nations as part of a real politic pogrom. These learned and legal gargoyles that are spawned also owe their origins to adhere to the so-called hegemonic and the so-called neo-imperialistic appellations, attached to the United States, as, it is known to have taken some harsh decisions, in the line of its humanitarian duties.

Iraq in 1991 and 2003, Vietnam, Korea and others, were decisions to pre-empt the war mongering of juntas that were taken-in tandem with the larger global community. International Law is very clear in its rendering despite wide and meandering interpretations that pre-emptive war with the sanctions and being within the ambit of the UN Charter, sanctions pre-emptive war, if adroitly sanctioned by the world body. Though it can be ascertained with some degree of academic grit that international organizations, world bodies and significant multilateral forums, will have to be 10 times more proactive, resourceful and creative if the philanthropic function of sustained world order has to be institutionalized.

But, here still, the leadership role falls in the court of America as it is the most powerful nation on the face of the international system, going by an economic, military and strategic reading of the superstate that the United States has become after the series of interventions in the international sphere. If one goes into a reading of the formulation of the UN Charter, the nations have sacrificed their selves and taken outstanding stand points in order to functionalize a corrective and peace-building system premised in the notion of collective security and pre-emption. Thus, pre-emption is part and parcel of the fundamental premise of the global war doctrines and strategizing as part of the theme of the net provisions of security and stealth in the international system. The United States by a stroke of chance - philanthropy happens to be the oracle - regulator of the selfsame.

The contemporary context is mired by the challenges faced by the preventive military doctrines that have been championed by the United States. Michael Eisenstadt writes for the Washington Institute, For some U.S. policymakers and military planners, Israel's 1981 raid on Iraq's Osiraq nuclear reactor may serve as an object lesson regarding the potential benefits of preventive military action against Iran's nuclear program. Not widely appreciated is how risky and difficult the Osiraq raid was, and how the factors which ensured its success make attempting similar action against Iran's nuclear facilities so challenging. U.S. preventive action against Iran's nuclear program would necessarily bear little resemblance to the Osiraq raid, and the results would unlikely be as decisive and lasting.[4]

We live in an age characterized by Kim Dong Un of North Korea coming through as the Dictator par excellence. The idea is that akin to the Osiraq nuclear reactor raid by Israel and the Entebbe raid carried on by the Mossad, the United States under the monitoring of President Barrack Obama went ahead with the idea of terminating Osama Bin Laden in the city of Abottabad right under the sniffing nose of the Pakistan's military establishment. Thus, the idea is that Preventive Diplomacy too takes the shape and contours of war-in-advance in order to take the aid of boots on the ground, to win over the foe or to counter a hard-nosed dictator or a military/communist junta. Thus, sniffing an enemy act has to do with the idiom of forecasting the ides of war, annihilation and perfidious perdition at the hands of a foe.

Iran might be construed as another facet of Pre-emptive war, where-in the United States might adapt an incursive mould, with the States forces undertaking a clean-up raid over Iran's nuclear installations such as Bushehr, Natanz and Ahvaz. It is further argued by Michael in the piece by the Washington Institute,

> Iran's nuclear program has made steady progress. The power plant at Bushehr is finally approaching completion. According to Russian officials, Unit I at Bushehr may be completed by late 2003 or early 2004, with the first consignment of reactor fuel to be delivered during this timeframe.6 Problems have dogged Iran's nuclear program from its inception. Russia originally undertook to complete Unit I by 1999, though technical and financial problems caused repeated delays. It is conceivable that new technical snafus, a Russian decision to hold-up the shipment of reactor components or fuel, or teething problems during reactor start-up, could further delay completion of the project. Iranian officials have indicated, however, that the successful completion of Unit I might lead to contracts for additional nuclear power plants at Bushehr and Ahvaz, providing a powerful incentive for continued Russian cooperation. Bushehr provides Iran with two potential routes to the Bomb.[5]

It is reported in the *Washington Post*,

> Though neither Iran nor Hizbollah are known to have directly targeted U.S. personnel or interests since the 1996 Khobar Towers bombing, Iran is keeping its options open: Iranian agents surveil U.S. personnel and installations from time to time, and Hizbollah retains a significant presence and support infrastructure in the United States that could be used to mount terrorist attacks on the United States. Moreover, U.S. officials recently claimed that al-Qaida officials in Iran were involved in the planning for the May 2003 bombings of three residential compounds in Riyadh, Saudi Arabia, that killed 25 (not including the nine bombers.[6]

Thus, Iran might be a future target that will entail an American special forces raid inside the terrain of the nation state of Iran. Effective intelligence too leads to productive fallouts for countries such as United States, where-in the confrontation can be gut wrenching and maladies excel in the foe, which would be Iran in the present context. Thus, Iran too is a target par excellence for a future and a post-truth Middle East/West Asia with the American superstate leading the torch of state-sponsored guerrilla histrionics with substance, of course.

The United States is bound to rely on naval platforms in order to circumvent the Iranian brigades and its various installations. Clifford Beal writes,

> The mission is likely to rely on naval platforms capable of launching Tomahawk land-attack cruise missiles (TLAMS) and strike aircraft against targets in southern and central Iran, while Air Force B-52s and B-2 stealth bombers operating from the continental United States would likely be tasked to strike targets deep in Iran (e.g., near Tehran). Range would not be a problem, and providing they achieve surprise, U.S. forces would stand a good chance of avoiding losses at the hands of Iranian air defences.[7]

As part of the pre-emptive strategy in Iran, it can be further said that

> Nearly all fixed wing fighter aircraft in the U.S. Naval and Air Force inventory can deliver precision munitions, and the United States has a number of conventional penetrator munitions (such as the GBU-28 laserguided bomb and the AGM-86D Conventional Air-Launched Cruise Missile Block III) for use against hardened and/or buried facilities. The Natanz centrifuge facility will reportedly be hardened

> and buried—protected by several meters of reinforced concrete and buried some 75 feet underground when completed.[8]

Thus, presaging and prologuing a full blown out conflict can be the future order of the day in the American art of conflict management.

The era of covert operations is still not over as the Americans will have to be true for their sage morality that is intertwined with pragmatic global concerns with a stout bearing on the American homeland dynamics. It can be surmised that "Covert action would probably be the most politically expedient way for the United States to disrupt Iran's nuclear program'. It might include one or more of the following measures, including the following:

- Harassment or murder of key Iranian scientists or technicians;
- Introduction of fatal design flaws into critical reactor, centrifuge or weapons components during their production, to ensure catastrophic failure during use[9];
- Disruption or interdiction of key technology or material transfers through sabotage or covert military actions on land, in the air or at sea;
- Sabotage of critical facilities by US intelligence assets, including third-country nationals or Iranian agents with access to key facilities;
- Introduction of destructive viruses into Iranian computer systems controlling the production of components or the operation of facilities;
- Damage or destruction of critical facilities through sabotage or direct action by US special forces.[10]

Thus, American covert operations still remain the stereotypical and trademark act of response by the Americans in conflict zones such as Iran, Iraq and Syria. Sabotage and subterfuge are also the key drivers with the inputs from intelligence, and the legerdemain of tact and planning will be the corner stone of an American riposte on Iran and other such recalcitrant state.

The *Daily Mail* has reported that even Vladimir Putin has erupted with his riposte against North Korea in the light of the novae linklight with the United States. The *Daily Mail* reported in March 2017,

> Vladimir Putin has warned **Kim Jong-Un** to stop threatening to launch nuclear weapons on foreign powers, as it could create 'a legal basis' for military action against **North Korea**. The Russian warning followed a call by Kim for his military to be prepared to mount pre-emptive attacks

> against the U.S and South Korea and stand ready to use nuclear weapons. U.S. and South Korean troops began large-scale military drills this week, which the North called 'nuclear war moves' and threatened to respond with an all-out offensive.[11]

The entire international community, at least the larger sections of the world, including state and non-state actors, have realized the significance of isolating the 'annoying nations'. The rationale for military incursions in the light of the liberal–democratic order still needs to be established with the larger comity of nations, their domestic public opinion and in the utterings of their leaders and diplomatists.

In a way, the nations that partake in blackmailing strategies, such as North Korea, need to be controlled and managed and if the civilized overtures do not work, then pre-emptive prevention through military is, normally, one of the options that are left. One notion still academically rules the roost that myriad nations can only be limited, covert and constrained in their preventive military measures keeping in view the general lacunae in the sovereignty debates in the international organizational fold and within the public spheres of the various nations. William J Perry calls it the 'Preventive Defense'. Political action and will can be the real harbingers of the peacenik approach amongst the polity of nations as Preventive Diplomacy can be granted a fuller role in determining the preventive acts of war in the service of conflict management. It has been noted,

> Political experience in preventive diplomacy provides a richer, but largely under-utilized, source of information. It has been pointed out that theory and generic knowledge are usually more helpful in the diagnosis of specific problems than in providing prescriptions for action. Theory and knowledge may, however, contribute to policy prescriptions when couched in terms of conditional generalizations which identify: the conditions that favor successful use of each particular instrument and strategy, and other conditions that make success very unlikely.[12]

Apart from rooting for the prevention of conflict scenarios, it can be ascertained that a more fulsome approach would be the eradication of the premised roots of conflict. Conflict prevention can have different targets. The most comprehensive approach would target the root causes of violence. According to this view, 'A comprehensive preventive strategy must first focus on the underlying political, social, economic, and environmental causes of conflict'.[13]

Thus, a framework or something that I refer to as the mainframe of conflict prevention, too, creates such a scenario that pre-emptive military action, too, becomes a part and parcel of the larger dynamics of conflict prevention. It is here the coalitions of nations can play a greater and legitimizing role for great powers such as Soviet Union, United States, China and the Indian Union in the trail of interventions.

Various nations make the target state stem the rot by traversing the roadmap from deterrence to corpulence. Schelling writes,

> In a deterrence relationship, the preventing actor communicates to the target that the violation of a norm would result, either because of denial or punishment, in major costs. While deterrence is a status quo policy, compellence requires an initiative by which the behavior of the target is altered. Compellence is a riskier behavior which is, after the failure of deterrence in the first place, continued "until the other acts rather than if he acts.[14]

It is this idiom of compellence that the United States and Israel know for their adventurism in the right domain for equalling the material, collateral damage that they suffer at the hands of State actors and terror actors. Thus, when deterrence fails, then the modicum of compellence and pre-emptive action, has to be adopted by the larger nation as the United States of America does.

Use of Force has been an instrument of pre-emptive warfare going by the tradition of the UN Charter. Looking through the prism of International Law, the entire theme of pre-emptive warfare is well debated and well established as a strategic doctrine that has been repeatedly and adroitly followed by the United States of America. Anthony Clark Arend writes,

> International law is created through the consent of states. States express this consent by two basic methods: treaties and custom. Treaties are written agreements between states; in effect, they are the international equivalent of contracts. Bilateral treaties are concluded between two states, such as the Strategic Arms Reduction Treaty between the United States and Russia and multilateral treaties are negotiated among many states, such as the UN Charter.[15]

Thus, the consent of the myriad nations and the leadership of a superstate, are the much needed requirements for the reaching of a collective understanding.The various nations have to be aligned against a 'Rogue Nation';

only then the entire notion and the intent of forestalling an attack on the homeland can be achieved.

The comity of nations can go ahead with a consensual understanding. The aggressive intent and the 'telling' acts of the Washington denomination can be perceived as a customary international law, which is different. Customary international law is coined and practiced as practical state practice, where-in what dominant and powerful nations such as the United States undertake becomes the standard policy vastly followed by the entire comity of states. Anthony Clark writes,

> Unlike treaties, customary international law is not created by what states put down in writing but, rather, by what states do in practice. In order for there to be a rule of customary international law, there must be an authoritative state practice. In order words, states must engage in a particular activity and believe that such activity is required by law. Diplomatic immunity, for example, began as a rule of customary international law before it was ultimately codified in a treaty. Centuries ago, states began the practice of granting diplomats immunity from local jurisdiction for a variety of pragmatic reasons: they did not wish to cut off a channel of communication; they feared that, if they arrested diplomats of a foreign state, the foreign state would do the same to their diplomats; and so on.[16]

One can historically align with the founding myth of the United Nations, where-in nations adhere to the global rule of law, if there is any such element in the international system. Collectively, the global nations endeavoured to lift the world out of the shadows of war and attrition through various means, where the consensual self-defence and forecasting the 'hurt potential' of a rogue nation were promptly taken into practical consideration. As an epistolary evidence, it can be quoted,

> As the Second World War was coming to an end, the delegates from 51 states assembled in San Francisco in the spring of 1945 to draft the charter of the new global organization. Pledging to 'save succeeding generations from the scourge of war,'6 the framers of the UN Charter sought to establish a normative order that would severely restrict the resort to force. Under Article 2(4) of the charter, states were to 'refrain in their international relations from the threat or use of force against the territorial integrity or political independence of any State or in any other manner inconsistent with the Purposes of the United Nations'.[17]

In the charter, there were only two explicit exceptions to this prohibition: force authorized by the Security Council and force in self-defence. The norm of peace was thus envisaged to be followed promptly and adroitly in a manner conducive to the non-restful and turbulent spirit of the international system after the end of World War II. The world wanted to awaken in the halo of a peaceful environment, which included the practice of forestalling conflict with or without the presence of rogue nations.

The question that can be asked repeatedly and with uncanny regularity and strategic aplomb, is, that if a series of humanitarian interventions have occurred, then have they been sanctioned by the UNSC. Although commentators may differ on the precise uses of force that have violated the UN Charter framework, the following list would seem to represent the kinds of force that have been used against the political independence and territorial integrity of states, have not been authorized by the Security Council and cannot be placed within any reasonable conception of self-defence: the Soviet action in Czechoslovakia (1948); the North Korean invasion of South Korea (1950); US actions in Guatemala (1954); the Israeli,[18] French and British invasion of Egypt (1956); the Soviet invasion of Hungary (1956); the US-sponsored Bay of Pigs invasion (1961); the Indian invasion of Goa (1961); the US invasion of the Dominican Republic (1965); the Warsaw Pact invasion of Czechoslovakia (1968); the Arab action in the 1973 Six-Day War; North Vietnamese actions against South Vietnam (1960–1975); the Vietnamese invasion of Kampuchea (1979); the Soviet invasion of Afghanistan (1979); the Tanzanian invasion of Uganda (1979); the Argentine invasion of the Falklands (1982); the US invasion of Grenada (1983); the US invasion of Panama (1989); the Iraqi attack on Kuwait (1990) and the NATO/US actions against Yugoslavia in the Kosovo situation (1999).[19] Still, all said and done, the International Regulator and a Coordinator-Leader is the requirement of the day which the United States can function as quite diligently. US being amongst the top three economies of the world and all glowing details shared in the CIA factbook can serve as a do gooder nation State or a nation with a well writ large philanthropic verve. This can concretise the world's response to non-state threats such as Terrorism, Insurgency, ill mounted wars of self determination and narratives crouching away surreptitiously from the ambit of nationalism and the sovereign lore of the nation. The mantle of leadership and cleansing thus falls in the lap of the nation on Mount Sinai.

What has to be understood in the entire deliberation is the factoid of the existence of WMDs and the practice and menace of terrorism. Article 2(4) that warns the nations against the use of force or even a threat of force also does not qualify the United States as the modicum of foreign policy and international relations (IR) and world politics, as I utilize these words interchangeably. Right from the days of the Kellogg–Briand Pact and the League of Nations, the various nations have acknowledged the "scourge of war" that recognized the menace of conflict in the documental form in the UN Charter.

With the new aspects of WMDs and the global war on terror, the procedural norms of the UN Charter and the globally regimental understanding of the 'Use of Force' has to be revisited in the larger international framework. Anthony Clark Arend writes in the *Washington Quarterly*,

> The lack of a new standard for preemptive force may not be the greatest challenge facing international law dealing with the recourse to force. As indicated above, most scholars addressing the current status of international law dealing with the preemptive use of force would argue that the law can be understood as being embodied in the UN Charter paradigm as modified slightly by customary international law. Hence, most scholars would conclude that the use of force is prohibited unless it has been authorized by the Security Council or is undertaken in self-defense.[20]

Thus, the issue of UNSC sanctioning the use of force is central to the entire discussion premised upon the treatment to be meted out to the rogue nations and other non-state outfits such as insurgents and various terrorist organizations.

Some of the nations have been calibrated as the 'Rogue Nations'. These nations are of the order of Libya, Iraq, North Korea, Iran and Sudan that fall out with the mainframe line of thought and categorization within the global comity of states. It's the alternate, irresponsible and aggressive state practice that is termed as the 'rogue behaviour' that refers to the idiom of rogue nations that do not adhere to the mainframe laws of standard state practice. The concept of rogue nations also emanates from the quintessential Bush doctrine in the aftermath of the September 11 attacks on the World Trade Organization. Christopher Preble at the Cato Institute writes, 'The lovable rogue is one of the most enduring archetypes of literature. From Robin Hood to Rhett Butler, some renegades who operate outside the bounds of acceptable behavior are nevertheless embraced as heroes because their intentions are good. In other words, they break the rules for good reasons and, in the process, win both admiration and affection'.[21] The Robinhoods of the age of yore in the Old World of continental Europe are the terror mongers of the contemporary world, where-in the impoverished rebels take up cudgels against the idiom of State domination that might not be actually inimical to the welfarist aspect of the domestic population. The idiom as always is that the rich classes and the ruling elites can be suppressed and their bag of riches can be distributed to the commoners, thus earning a permanent support system for the rebel par excellence. Thus, the same metaphor applies to the resurgence of the rogue states, the pariah states and the outlaw states, and the traditional and emblematic usurper, that is, the United States of America. They don't intend the Americans to be the Sheriff and the Peace Pontiff in an Oregon trail gone awry in the path to progress, regulation and glory. US has to be functional as a Global regulator, come what may. It's the tryst with destiny with New Delhi being a copartner in the context of the Pulwama attack.

Still, when the aid and sanction of the UNSC is talked about, the UNSC sanction can be the arbiter of the dispute surrounding the 'Use of Force'. Preble further writes, 'The Secretary General's High-Level Panel on Threats, Challenges and Change expanded on this theme in its 2004 report, A More Secure World: Our Shared Responsibility. The Security Council, the panelists explained, could authorize "military intervention as a last resort, in the event of genocide and other large-scale killing, ethnic cleansing or serious violations of humanitarian law"'.[22] Thus, humanitarian law enters the paradigm of R2P, when, the legalities of the use of force are delved inside with some detail. Abraham Lincoln also contended that 'Those who deny the freedom of life, expression and larger montage to the people just know by the Justice of God that their individual freedom too can be eviscerated and taken away from them'. Still, the United Nations can be said to restrain the various nations from the pre-emptive acts of war and directs the various states to go across the vestibule in the United Nations and seek the permission of the Security Council along with utilizing the military and the defence option as the 'last option and the last resort', when all diplomatic instruments have been eroded away and the talks do not lead to a solution in the ides of conflict management. Still, state practice and the idealist notions of a UN-ordained peacenik behavioural morality cannot be a safe and often-followed facet of the international system. Behavioural uncertainties are a norm of the comity of states and it is this facet and characteristic of the world system that promptly militates against the *nom de plume* of International Law, and what can the Global commons do, is anybody's guess.

State practice is often arbitrary and unpredictable, akin to the behaviour of the non-state actors in a largely ruleless, lawless, chaotic, pandemonium inclined and an anarchic world system, where, the writ of powerful and the well-accoutred rules the roost. Thus, the iota of a 'mistook war' can every now and then overwhelm the peace and stability of the larger international system. Self-interested and national interest–centric state behaviour is the perennial and persistent order of the day. The nations also forgo the principles and tenets of international law and act in a self-seeking, egoistic and systemic manner, such as Iraq and Pakistan in order to win in a zero-sum-game system of the global polity akin the game theory of economics and IR theory. Such is the framework of the anarchic world order, where several nations flout the norm setting of international law and go scot-free after committing acts of genocide, ethnic cleansing and other flagrant violations of the law's cannon in the international system.

Powerful and well-accoutred nations have been known to be realist 'play actors', where-in the superstates with their hyperpuissance, such as the pelf of United States of America, tend to pip most of the other states and non-state actors to the post. Thus, when America plays the role of the international balancer and monitor of the class of international actors, it is surprising that myriad eyebrows are raised on its intent and strategic inclination. In a multilateral world order, despite academic misgivings, the charge of the light brigade lies with an omniscient United States with its all-pervading grasp over the larger sinews of the international system.

Randall L Schweller writes in an Oxford publication,

> The balance of power—a notoriously slippery, murky, and protean term, endlessly debated and variously defined—is the core theory of international politics within the realist perspective. A 'balance of power' system is one in which the power held and exercised by states within the system is checked and balanced by the power of others. Thus, as a nation's power grows to the point that it menaces other powerful states, a counter-balancing coalition emerges to restrain the rising power, such that any bid for world hegemony will be self-defeating.[23]

The author further contends, 'The minimum requirements for a balance of power system include the existence of at least two or more actors of roughly equal strength, states seeking to survive and preserve their autonomy, alliance flexibility, and the ability to resort to war if need be'.[24] Thus, one of the long-term consequences of an American balancer and a leader role to be more precise, can be the idiom that the multilateral crowd of nations can congeal and spawn a conglomerate around the rising hegemon and the superstate of the times, such as United Kingdom and France a couple of centuries back, and nations such as America that rule the international roost in a post-truth and post-recession world in the contemporary context. In a way, the American idiom of the day contends that multilateralism is a mere façade with the alternate power centres capable of balancing the United States, but in the 21st century, the United States will remain the power zone of the world for future decades to come.

Joseph Grieco, the IR scholar contends,

> Within an anarchic realm, which lacks a sovereign arbiter to make and enforce agreements among states, there must be at least two states that seek self-preservation, above all, for a balance of power to exist. Further, states must be more self-interested than group-interested. Each desires, if possible, greater power than its neighbors. If states act to promote the long-run community interest over their short-run national interest (narrowly defined), or if they equate the two sets of interests, then they exist within either a Concert system or a Collective Security system. Simply put, states in a balance of power system are not altruistic or other-regarding. They act, instead, in ways that maximize their relative gains and avoid or minimize their relative losses.[25]

Thus, bilateralism comes into being, where-in the twin key antagonistic nations in the larger world are pitted against each other. The nations attempt to minimize their self-interested and self-seeking objectives in order to garner relative gains. In a way, the powerful nation state actor such as United States would embalm itself with the blood of the prime antagonist and then will attempt to neutralize or balance out the other power pole in the international system. Or else, to utilize fanciful language, the nation can eulogize itself and canonize oneself with the anointment of the universal do-gooder state on a celestial pathway to renew and revitalize the international comity of States. Even, 'bamboozling' the Rogue nations and the larger hostile world can be another solution and an ideal way out, if, nations such as the United States have to sustain their world dominance while playing service to the 'challenged' states and regions of the world. The idiom of dominance also involves the instrumentality of alter-casting and reification, where-in one nation state lives the alter image of the antagonist in the aftermath of a détente.

In the words of the IR observers, the entire international system can be divided into three segments akin to Morton Kaplan's World Systems approach. The three world orders running alternate to each other are of the following order:

- **A negotiated order.** A rule-based order that is the result of a grand bargain voluntarily struck among the major actors who, therefore, view the order as legitimate and beneficial.[26] It is a highly institutionalized order, ensuring that the hegemon will remain engaged in managing the order, but will not exercise its power capriciously. In this way, a negotiated rule-based order places limits on the returns to power, especially with respect to the hegemon. Pax Americana (1945–present) and, to a lesser extent, Pax Britannica (19th century) are exemplars of this type of 'liberal constitutional' order.
- **An imposed order.** A non-voluntary order among unequal actors purposefully designed and ruled by a malign (despotic) hegemon, whose power is unchecked. The Soviet satellite system is an exemplar of this type of order.[27]
- **A spontaneously generated order.** Order is an unintended consequence of actors seeking only to maximize their interests and power. It is an automatic or self-regulating system. Power is checked by countervailing power, thereby placing limits on the returns to power. The classic 18th-century European balance of power is an exemplar of this type of order.[28] Thus, the negotiated order happens to be the one which works in the contemporary world, but it is here that nations such as the United States fulfil their predestination. The entire global amity of states would be organized in a recalibration by the United States due to its larger pelf, might and being a leader and fore-runner of the network society and the larger international system. The US thus emerges as a non-hegemonic and alternate world regulator, despite the sovereign reservations of the lesser abled and 'challenged' multiple nation state players in the larger world system.

The United States of America has emerged as 'the Regulator nation' since the dawn of the 20th century with the understanding that its internal girth is responsible for its dominance and supersession to a higher power perch in a hot, flat and overcrowded world where newly emergent actors are jostling for power and influence peddling. Multipolarity is here to stay in the form of nations such as People's Republic of China, Russia, Japan, Brazil, Japan and others, with the Asiatic space emerging as the contested mainframe of the world instead of being a margin of the larger international system.

In such a contested terrain populated by the unilateralists and the multilateralists, bandwagoning happens to be the skit for survival where-in, the various nations go ahead with jettisoning older bargains and coalitions and hitching a ride with the powerful bloc or the *au courant* superstate. Walt writes in the same context, 'There have been several recent challenges to the conventional realist wisdom that balancing is more prevalent than bandwagoning behavior, that is, when states join the stronger or more threatening side'.[29] The author further contends,

> Paul Schroeder's broad historical survey of international politics shows that states have bandwagoned with or hid from threats far more often than they have balanced against them. Similarly, I have claimed that bandwagoning behavior is more prevalent than contemporary realists have led us to believe because alliances among revisionist states, whose behavior has been ignored by modern realists, are driven by the search for profit, not security.[30]

The various scholars have differently poised but quaintly converging standpoints pertaining to the question of comprehending the pelf and power of the stealthy world power such as the United States of America. In a way, G H Snyder contends, 'Parenthetically, alliance handicaps explain why the alliance flexibility that seemingly derives from the wealth of physical alternatives theoretically available under a multipolar structure should not be confused with the actual alternatives that are politically available to states within the system given their particular interests and affinities'.[31] The United States of America carries this quality that conveniently qualifies it for the seat of world regulation and balancing as the networked strength of United States' diplomacy is as pertinent as the outlandish military and economic strength of the nation. Thus, the coalition-building inclination and propensities in the context of the United States hold pre-eminence in the larger power dynamics of America in the light of an international system chugging along peacefully to an egalitarian and equity-driven principle. Stephen Brooks and William Wohlforth see a world out of balance—one in which the United States maintains its unchallenged global primacy for another 20 years or more.[32]

It can also be contended,

> The US has the most technologically powerful economy in the world, with a per capita GDP of $54,800. US firms are at or near the forefront in technological advances, especially in computers, pharmaceuticals, and medical, aerospace, and military equipment; however, their advantage has narrowed since the end of World War II. Based on a comparison of GDP measured at Purchasing Power Parity conversion rates, the US economy in 2014, having stood as the largest in the world for more than a century, slipped into second place behind China, which has more than tripled the US growth rate for each year of the past four decades.[33]

The Central Intelligence Agency *World Factbook* contends,

> In the US, private individuals and business firms make most of the decisions, and the federal and state governments buy needed goods and services predominantly in the private marketplace. US business firms enjoy greater flexibility than their counterparts in Western Europe and Japan in decisions to expand capital plant, to lay off surplus workers, and to develop new products. At the same time, businesses face higher barriers to enter their rivals' home markets than foreign firms face entering US markets.[34] Thus, the primacy of Industry along with the idiom of being a powerful economy makes the United States a favourite leader of the comity of nations in the present times along with being a fore runner in the near future as the United States after its economic downturn has ably recalibrated its power turnstiles and become a daring and innovating nationality under the suzerainty of President Trump. These factual indicators cast aspersions upon the forecasts of the 'naysayers' as the United States seems poised to be the world leader in the larger picture of the international system with its giant economy, military strength and the canny verve of its geo-strategic pelf in the larger, 'Realm'.

International and Non-International Armed Conflicts: The New Warring Paradigm

Since the World War II, most of the civil wars, which are the paradigmatic notions about non-international armed conflicts (NIACs) and are tantamount to a majority of all armed conflicts, have gained in currency and popularity as part of the popular lore with the idea that most of these civil wars have been home to foreign nation interventions. It might be considered that are the involved nations in the arm of the territorial party in the civil war or on the side of the non-state rogue actor in the civil war. The legal impact of such foreign interventions may result in parallel armed conflicts taking place in the same territory resulting in the internationalization of the NIAC between a territorial state and a non-state group and a reclassification of hostilities between a territorial state and a foreign state from an international armed conflict (IAC) to an NIAC.[35]

Moreover these interventions also raise various general and important questions regarding conflict classification in International Humanitarian Law (IHL). Wilmshurst writes in her work, 'Most of these questions have been discussed and deliberated in great detail by the scholars, intellectuals and international tribunals but they have not been accorded enough academic attention in the sphere of International Relations'.[36]

The issues of the legality and the legal tenability of the interventions by European powers such as by France inside Mali with the invitation by the legal Government of Mali can be an instance that foreign interventions in an NIAC are matters of global and norm-setting concerns. Similarly, the issue of the United States of America intervening in nations such as Korea, Philippines, Cuba, Vietnam, Panama, Grenada and Nicaragua can be other instances where-in the legality of these interventions can occupy the academic concerns of IL experts and other IR observers. Thus, several states such as Mexico, Burma and Russia have already expressed their disinterest and disagreement with the conventions such as the Geneva Conventions Additional Protocols and the original case law being derived out of the entire edifice of IHL. These three nations have vociferously contested the idea that IHL applies to these interventions, but the flip side also contends that going by the tribunals, such as International Criminal Tribunal on Yugoslavia (ICTY) and International Criminal Tribunal on Rwanda (ICTR), involving Rwanda and Yugoslavia, the non-state actors such as terror and insurgent groups are also responsible for the humanitarian situations in their respective conflict zones.[37]

Also, several non-state actors and the rogue actors, have to be associated with an iota of intensity and the degree of conflict along with expressing some degree of organization in their ranks including a semblance of organizational structure and a section of command and control. Al Qaeda, ISIS and Al-Nusra Front might escape being the terror organizations if these above-written norms cannot be applied to them. Thus, even terrorist organizations, can, seek a leeway out of the norm setting of international law if some iota of 'prescribed pedigree' is not found inside their organizations.

It can be contended that 'extensive and virtually uniform' and combined with *opinio juris*, state practice creates customary rules. State practice is an important factor when interpreting Treaty Law. One fact can be asserted that a proper analysis of state practice is absent from the *nom de plume* of IHL practice.[38] States do not classify their wars as IACs or NIACs, but rather call the myriad wars as 'Operations' such as Operation Urgent Fury, Operation Just Cause, Operation Restore Hope, Operation Enduring Freedom, Operation Deny Flight and Operation Desert Storm. Pakistan in Pulwama too crossed the rubicon and was punished by a Mirage-2000 clean up act of terror camps in Pakistan occupied Kashmir lately.

The term "Armed Conflict" is not defined in the Geneva conventions or in the Additional Protocols.[39] The ICTY commented that 'there is a resort to Armed Force between states'. It fails to explicitly state that the resort to Armed Force between states must be connected to differences, and to disputes between states. The requirement of a dispute between states should not be interpreted as requiring that we examine the attention of the actors behind every act of hostilities. It should be used only in order to exclude consensual use of Armed Force by states in the territory of other states.

There is a requirement of an intensity of the conflict even in an IAC. For instance, the UK military manual states, 'Whether any particular intervention crosses the threshold so as to become an armed conflict, will depend upon all the surrounding circumstances. For example, the rejecting of border police with soldiers or any accidental border incursion by members of Armed forces would not, in itself, amount to an armed conflict'.[40] Thus, the practices are all about state practices that have not been provided amply gateways and leeway in the *nom de plume* of the International Treaty mechanisms where IHL takes its own toll on the parties to the conflict and normally assumes an anti State and anti nationalistic rubric..

Robert Colb refers to the nomenclature of the IACs,

> Such troops between United Nations Troops or troops of any other international organizations, and local forces always trigger the

> application of the law international armed conflict. UN operations by their very nature are international. They are decided on the basis of international policy; their mandate is typically international; they are conducted by a principle of International Law across the boundaries of a state. Therefore, armed conflict is internationalized. The afore-mentioned aspects of rationae materiae and rationae personae trigger the application of the Law of international armed conflict.[41]

Thus, once even international actors of the order of the United States, too, enter the centrestage in some internal conflict, akin to the involvement of the United Nations, the American entry inside the civil wars also leads to the idiom of the internationalization of that particular conflict with attendant vituperations germinating about Washington's avowed national interest and so forth.

Still, the state practice is always found to be observing the working and the principle of IHL. It is written that,

> International Humanitarian Law is no way Lex Specalis to the law of State responsibility; the issue of the qualification of the legal nature of an armed conflict is solely one for International Humanitarian Law; and has nothing to do with the law of State responsibility, even though the factual patterns on which these branches of law operate might be very similar.[42]

These interpretations of IHL sometimes end up fallaciously devouring the national interest oriented locus standi of the State actors.In many instances, direct military interventions are not the only qualification for the spawning of an IAC. In the Nicaragua case, the International Court of Justice (ICJ) stated that the US and Nicaragua were involved in an IAC with each other. The reasoning in support of that conclusion, was however, quite unclear: 'As Nicaragua is not easy reading, and there are various interpretations of the judgment of the International Court of Justice'.[43] One plausible interpretation is that 'By the mere act of Arming and Training the contras, the organs of US not only violated the prohibition on the use of Force in jus ad bellum but also used armed force to an extent that triggered IHL'. Thus, the American cause in the intervention in the State of Nicaragua was not to become the internationally celebrated 'Just Cause' as the external use of the instruments of training, arming and advising the Contras against the Nicaraguan Government happened to be a universally culpable act that was undertaken by the US in order to fulfil its national interest.

In the same manner, there has always been a rampant effort from the fence-side of the purveyor nations of a multilateral world order. Here the smaller and undeveloped states tend to create an exclusionary Regime of Treaty Law and the larger rubric of norm setting in the context of International Law.

Adam Bower writes in his book on the non–great power states,

> The international community frequently incorporates variety of concessions to facilitate Great Power engagement, thereby, limiting the scope of legally binding rules. This has been perceived in the long term efforts to regulate small arms and light weapons that recently culminated in the recently concluded Arms Trade Treaty, (ATT). The same underlying rule pinpoints that great powers tend to derail the process of rules and regulations and the Global Regimes such as the Treaties for Global norms in the spheres of Climate Change, Arms reduction, human rights and Disarmament.[44]

Nations such as China, Russia, India and Brazil too espouse the idea that the context of multilateralist attempts and strivings by the non–great power nations is a way to be in the exclusive club of nations such as United States and United Kingdom. Also, nations such as the United States have not ratified the Mine Ban Treaty and the International Criminal Court (ICC) treaties that their domestic legislative establishments have found to be inappropriate for their national interests and far off from the regime of consensual decision making in the domestic realms of their various nations.

As an instance, in the early hours of 18 July 1998, in the large Plenary Halls of the UN Food and Agriculture Organization in Rome, the delegates to the UN group of diplomatic plenipotentiaries, convened for the voting objectives for the final draft of the ICC. The tirade was directed against the plethora of powerful states and the other club of victors in the aftermath of World War II. It is mentioned,

> The Committee of the whole assembled at first in the Red Room, in this cramped and inconvenient space with too few states, representatives of NGO's and Government alike thronged the aisles and the seats. In the biggest and the most emotional demonstration of the evening, cheering, hugging, weeping and rhythmic applause followed a defeat of the American amendment in the Rome Statute by 113 votes. The intense reaction reflected a trenchant fear that even at the last minute the strenuous Diplomacy of the United States in Rome and its blunt

> bilateral maneuvers around the world would succeed either in putting the conference in impasse or in rendering largely impotent, the eventual Court.[45]

Thus, the non-act of United States of America, not to ratify the anti-mine legislation and the Rome Statute on ICC, led to the idiom of the bigger nations being sidelined in the larger rigmarole of the larger international system. The United States of America likens itself to be a philanthropic nation state, but in a manner and place-time of its own liking and choice. Washington works as a standard regulator nation state and very naturally, too, the, powerful and well-resourced nation states need to be burdened with the global responsibility to ensure the pelf, piety and the prosperity of the larger world that is not so well resourced and fortunately endowed as nations such as United States are, or, happen to be.

There is an expectation of great power leadership. The first factor, typical of all the factors of realism, expects that preponderantly powerful states will promote norms, laws and organizational forms that reflect their particular interests and thereby extend their dominance of the international system. What the proponents of the multilateral comity of nations need to comprehend that, it is the nom de plume or the fait accompli of the largely regulated world order. The condition of anarchy severely constrains the possibility of non-exploitative cooperation. Governance is consequently brittle and requires the continued deployment of coercive power to sustain it. To overcome this, hegemons and other leading powers offer inducements such as preferred security alliances or preferential trade agreements and threats including sanctions and military interventions in order to gain support for their preferred policies and sustain their influence in the larger international system. Still, this is a very natural and self styled prophesy in order to balance and equilibrate the largely morphing international system.

The relationship between norms and law can be taken up in the sense that law exists as a codified version of principles and values, while, the maxim of norms amounts to the larger rubric of deliberations and discussions. The starting point in the deliberations is that treaties should be conceptualized as focal points in the development of international norms, which can be defined conventionally as standards of appropriate behaviour that describe what types of actions are permissible or impermissible for actors in a particular context. Norms often lack codification in a written text, but, nonetheless exert an indelible influence in defining the acceptable type and range of actor behaviours and more fundamentally contribute to the constitution of their identities and interests.

Hart writes, 'The notion that law is underpinned by more fundamental normative commitments is in itself, not revealatory. It is generally recognized that particular systems of rules necessarily rely upon more fundamental principles and rules for their creation, interpretation, and modification'.[46] Thus, fundamental principles of law, order and a rules-based system lead to the idiom of creating organizing agents for making functional the larger altercations between myriad nationalities and their interests. Also, as an attendant fact, these rules-based change and ordering principles can only be equated with the powerful nations of the international system. The larger powers such as the United States serve as the de facto rules-based enforcers and the regulators par excellence, much to the 'chargin' of the critics in a manner that can be audible to the larger international system. The great powers in a way are the World War II traditionalists that are the purveyors of the destiny that manifests itself in the denouements to conflicts, the world over. Nations such as the United States, are the global arbiters that rule the roost over the larger world. Nations such as the United States akin to the Romans, Greeks, Incas and the Ottomans are the new world–order legerdemains of the 21st century that can question the excesses in conflict scenarios. Most of the nations bandwagon with them and it's a foolhardy policy to rebel against a conclave that is only striving to solve global and regional fracas and order a flagellating and fluctuating international system.

Traces of hegemony might be visible in this international state practice, but it's the time-travelled and hallowed Great power 'slouch' that makes the ordered international system go around. It is not akin to accommodating a gargantuan monster gone berserk in a closed mansion, where all the internalities are smudged over by the rotating tail of the monster that has been kept in a constrained role in the mansion. Thus, great powers such as the United States cannot be constrained as they do no good in such a delimited role. The requirement and the clamour of the day is that these nations need to be given a freedom to regulate and norm set the larger international comity in consonance with their 'Real power and Innocent clout and awesome aura'. It's not a bid to punctuate a multilateral order of new play actors, but, a proven reservoir of rationale to order the system and sustain the precariously poised balance of power system.

As an instance, the Rome Statute seeks to establish a new international norm considering an appropriate response to international crime. The international state practice according to the 'new norm setting' has to be such that states are now obliged to investigate and criminally sanction individual human beings for acts of atrocity, via a set of internationally negotiated judicial standards. By joining the Rome Statute, states also accepted a supranational body with the authority to conduct its own investigations and trials, and to evaluate and potentially intervene in international legal proceedings.[47] In this latter respect, the innovation of the Rome Statute concerns the willingness of states to turn over some measure of their sovereign rights to prosecute their nationals to a permanent international body over which they cannot exercise complete control. Though an international body, the Court required the active support of States to enact its requests for assistance and legal judgements leading to an enforcement problem at the heart of the ICC Regime.[48]

Though the United States is not a member of the Rome Statute, it opens itself up for charges of being a non-cooperative partner in the Global regime to sustain and spawn a narrative and an international law instrumentality against International crime by both state and non-state actors. What needs to be ascertained and informed is that even several African nations that are members of the African Union have not been adhering to the just and humane state practice, as, enshrined in the Rome Statute. Nations such as Kenya as a routinized ritual, express their adherence to the general norms of justice and fairness, ending impunity for grave crimes, and promoting the rule of law, along with support for an effective, impartial ICC.[49]

Still, nations in Africa, are, too home to a mandate of genocide and impunity. Still, the more rankling factor is the American disdain for entering inside the framework of the Rome Statute as a full-fledged member state. The Global Policy Forum informs,

> The United States government has consistently opposed an international court that could hold US military and political leaders to a uniform global standard of justice. The Clinton administration participated actively in negotiations towards the International Criminal Court treaty, seeking Security Council screening of cases. If adopted, this would have enabled the US to veto any dockets it opposed. When other countries refused to agree to such an unequal standard of justice, the US campaigned to weaken and undermine the court. The Bush administration, coming into office in 2001 as the Court neared implementation,

> adopted an extremely active opposition. Washington began to negotiate bilateral agreements with other countries, insuring immunity of US nationals from prosecution by the Court.[50]

The portal further informs,

> As leverage, Washington threatened termination of economic aid, withdrawal of military assistance, and other painful measures. The Obama administration has so far made greater efforts to engage with the Court. It is participating with the Court's governing bodies and it is providing support for the Court's ongoing prosecutions. Washington, however, has no intention to join the ICC, due to its concern about possible charges against US nationals.[51]

There is also an inclusion of the America Service Members Act that can be cited as a traditional American approach to International crime. It's been a tradition and a historical fact that the US establishment has gone ahead with the act and well-pronounced and partisan policy intent of protecting the lives and interests of its personnel, military personnel and foreign service missionaries even in the face of the concerns raised by other multilateralist votaries. What more can a nation do other than adhere to the rote but much required self oriented dictum of national interest, though there might be a further demarcation between, short term and long term national interests in the larger schemata of global developments.

Even in the recent test case in the context of the Libya and the statement of Susan Rice, a great deal of politics exist concerning the fate of recalcitrant nation state actors. Though the UNSC R 1973 clearly mentions that it is the ICC that is responsible for attempting action on Colonel Gaddafi, the American Representative, Susan Rice in 2011 championed the right and the prerogative of the Libyan people to try their leader. It is informed in the *Foreign Policy Journal*, 'Following US Ambassador to the UN Susan Rice's announcement that Libyan people can decide whether to try Gaddafi, the ICC chief prosecutor Luis Moreno-Ocampo released a statement reaffirming that the ICC, not Libya, must make the decision regarding Gaddafi's trial. These conflicting statements highlight background politics of the Security Council (SC) and international law'.[52]

The *Foreign Policy Journal* further cites the UNSC resolution contending,

> Under controversial Resolution 1973, the SC granted the ICC authority to prosecute top Libyan officials for their role in the bloody crackdown

> on protests, but recent statements by Rice and other P3 (UK, etc.) members of the council 'delegitimize' the role of the ICC. This shows the danger of the ICC being used by the SC in such an instrumental and political way.[53]

The *Foreign Policy Journal* too mentions that in the context of May 2017 that the drug carnage and the goon wars going on in Columbia needs to be controlled and if the ICC finds its hands tied, then the United States, being true to its regulator role, can intervene in the cascade of violence and turmoil in the nation state of Colombia. Thus, the idiom of interventionism still holds a debate and deliberation podium for itself and in the interest of fairness and just cause in carrying on International Politics in the larger international system. India's Air Force intervention in Balakot, Chikoti and Muzzafarabad, too is as a striving to neutralise the role of non-state terror actors. US might be an interventionist, but for a just cause.

NOTES

1. 'Chapter VII: UN Charter, Action With Respect to Threats to Peace, Breaches of the Peace, and Acts of Aggression'. http://www.un.org/en/sections/un-charter/chapter-vii/. Accessed 3 May 2017.
2. Ibid.
3. Ibid.
4. Eisenstadt, 'The Challenges of Preventive Military Action'. http://www.washingtoninstitute.org/policy-analysis/view/the-challenges-of-u.s.-preventive-military-action. Accessed 1 May 2018.
5. Ibid.
6. Preist, Dana and Susan Schmidtt, 'Al Waida Figure Tied to Riyadh Blasts', *The Washington Post*, 18 May 2003.
7. Beal, Clifford, Mark Hewish and Leland Ness, 'Hard Target Attack: Forging a Better Hammer', *International Defense Review*, 29, 1996, pp. 32-38; Sepp, Eric M., 'Deeply Buried Facilities: Implications for Military Operations', Air War College Center for Strategy and Technology, Occasional Paper No. 14, May 2000. http://www.au.af.mil/au/awc/awcgate/cst/csat14.pdf.
8. Ibid.
9. Ibid.
10. Ibid.
11. Malm, Sara. 'Putin Warns Kim Jong Un Against Preventive Nuclear Strikes', *Daily Mail*, 7 March 2017.
12. See Boutros-Ghali (1992) and Evans (1994). Recent UN preventive activities are reported in detail by Boutros-Ghali (1995). Evans' blueprint for preventive diplomacy is supported by several case studies in Clements and Ward (1994).
13. Commission on Global Governance, 1995.
14. Schelling, Thomas C., *The Strategy of Conflict*. Cambridge, MA: Harvard University Press, 1980.

15. Arend, Anthony Clark, 'International Law and the Preemptive Use of Military Force', *Washington Quarterly*, 2003.
16. Ibid.
17. Letter from Mr. Webster to Mr. Fox, 24 April 1841, cited in Damrosch et al., International Law: Cases and Materials, 2001.
18. Arend, Anthony C., and Rober J. Beck, *International Law and the Use of Force: Beyond the U.N. Charter Paradigm*, pp. 182–183.
19. Ibid.
20. Arend, op. cit.
21. Preble, Christopher, 'The Bush Doctrine and the Rogue States'. https://object.cato.org/sites/cato.org/files/articles/preble_afsa_bush_doctrine_rogue_states.pdf. Accessed 3 May 2018.
22. Ibid.
23. Schweller, Randall L., 'The Balance of Power in World Politics', *Politics: Oxford Research Encyclopedia.*
24. Ibid.
25. Grieco, Joseph M., *Cooperation Among Nations: Europe, America, and Non-tariff Barriers to Trade*. Ithaca, NY: Cornell University Press, 1990.
26. Ikenberry, G.J., *After Victory: Institutions, Strategic Restraint, and the Rebuilding of Order After Major Wars*. Princeton, NJ: Princeton University Press, 2001.
27. Ibid.
28. Ibid.
29. Walt, S.M.,*The Origins of Alliances*. Ithaca, NY: Cornell University Press, 1987.
30. Ibid.
31. Snyder, G.H., *Alliance Politics*. Ithaca, NY: Cornell University Press, 1997.
32. Wohlforth, W.C, The Stability of a Unipolar World. *International Security*, 1999.
33. The World Factbook: America, Central Intelligence Agency. https://www.cia.gov/library/publications/the-world-factbook/geos/us.html. Accessed 1 May 2017.
34. Ibid.
35. Zamir, Noam, Chapter, "Civil Wars and Insurgency," *Classification of Conflicts in International Humanitarian Law: The Legal impact of Foreign Intervention in Civil Wars*, Cheltanham, UK: Elgar Publishing, 2017, pp. 8-15.
36. Wilmshurst (ed.), *International Law and the Classification of Conflicts*, Oxford, UK: Oxford University Press, 2012.
37. Zamir, op. cit.
38. *North Sea Continental Shelf* cases (*Federal Republic of Germany v. Denmark*; *Federal Republic of Germany v. Netherlands*), Judgment, ICJ Reports, 1969; *Continental Shelf* (*Libyan Arab Jamahiriya v. Malta*), Judgment, ICJ Reports, 1985. Sivakumaran, S., *The Law of the Non-International Armed Conflict*, Oxford, UK: Oxford University Press, 2012.
39. *Prosecutor v. Tadic*, IT-94-AR 72, 2 October 1995, pp. 70, 184.
40. UK Ministry of Defense, *The Manual of the Law of Armed Conflict*, Oxford, UK: Oxford University Press, 2004.
41. Zamir, op. cit., pp. 199–200.
42. *The Application of the Convention on the Prevention and Punishment of the Crime of Genocide* (*Bosnia and Herzegovina v. Serbia and Montenegro*) Judgment, ICJ Reports, 2007.
43. *Military and Paramilitary Activities in and Against Nicaragua* (*Nicaragua v. US*), Merits, Judgment, ICJ Reports, 1986, p. 14.
44. Bower, Adam, *Norms Without the Great Powers: International Law and Changing Social Standards*

in World Politics, London: Oxford University Press, 2017, pp. 1–20.

45. Bendetti, Fanny, Karine Booniue and John Washburn, *Negotiating the International Criminal Court: New York to Rome*, Leiden: Martinus Nijhoff Publishers, p. 1.
46. Hart, H.L.A., *The Concept of Law*, 2nd ed. Oxford: Oxford University Press, 1994, pp. 1–15.
47. Mullins, Christopher W. and Dawn L. Rothe, 'The Ability of the International Criminal Court to Deter Violations of International Criminal Law: A Theoretical Assessment', *International Criminal Law Review*, 10(5), 2010, pp. 771–786.
48. Ibid.
49. Republic of Kenya 2013, Assembly of the African Union 2013, Republic of Uganda 2013; Kingdom of Lesotho 2014.
50. 'Global Policy Forum: US Opposition to the International Criminal Court'. https://www.globalpolicy.org/international-justice/the-international-criminal-court/us-opposition-to-the-icc.html. Accessed 1 May 2017.
51. Ibid.
52. Bosco, David. 'Susan Rice Versus the ICC Prosecutor', *Foreign Policy*, 24 August 2011.
53. Ibid.

6

The Nicaragua Case Study: The Unilateralist America or Else

AS a prominent case study, the United States of America has intervened in smaller issue nations in a preponderant adherence to its national interest. One of them happens to be Nicaragua. According to one reading of the scenario, it was the American aiding and abating the Contras against the Sandinista Government in Nicaragua since 1985 that led to the attack on American. Despite the American clout, the International Court of Justice (ICJ) expressed in its Advisory Opinion that 'United States standpoint and act of aiding the Contra Rebels were Ultra Vires of the norm setting of the Regime of International cooperation and Law'. But Washington came through with an outright rejection of the compulsory jurisdiction of the ICJ very much similar to what the Chinese standpoint is vis-à-vis the arbitration tribunal as created by the ICJ. Beijing, too, refused to accept the jurisdiction of the Arbitral Tribunal in the context of the South China sea disputes and the island sovereignty disputes with the smaller nations in the region, so, one must pinpoint that when the index finger is pointing towards others, the, the rest of the palm is pointing towards the alleger.

The panel of Judges at the ICJ decided that by 12 votes to 3, the American standpoint was found to be flawed and the United States was found to be the recalcitrant and the transgressor nation state. The final judgement of the ICJ can be quoted here from the judgement deliberations of the Court:

> *The Court contends that, 'Decides* that the United States of America, by training, arming, equipping, financing and supplying the *contra* forces

> or otherwise encouraging, supporting and aiding military and paramilitary activities in and against Nicaragua, has acted, against the Republic of Nicaragua, in breach of its obligation under customary international law not to intervene in the affairs of another State'.[1]
>
> *The Court contends that,* 'that the United States of America, by certain attacks on Nicaraguan territory in 1983-1984, namely attacks on Puerto Sandino on 13 September and 14 October 1983, an attack on Corinto on 10 October 1983; an attack on Potosi Naval Base on 4/5 January 1984, an attack on San Juan del Sur on 7 March 1984; attacks on patrol boats at Puerto Sandino on 28 and 30 March 1984; and an attack on San Juan del Norte on 9 April 1984; and further by those acts of intervention referred to in subparagraph (3) hereof which involve the use of force, has acted, against the Republic of Nicaragua, in breach of its obligation under customary international law not to use force against another State'.[2]

Thus, here we focus upon the operative part of the judgement that looks into the detailed and the factual part and parcel of the ICJ judgement. The general argument of the Court is that the United States of America had flouted the tenets of Customary International Law and the breach of the UN Charter through the abatement of threat and use of force finds Washington in the docks despite the clandestine nature of the American military operation.

The American literature talks about the streak of individualism and go-it-alone approach. What is significant to be noticed is the factoid that most of the Americans have not read Descartes and his academic thesis, but they all seem to be the followers of the quaint personage. What it means is that Americans believe in the idiom of entrepreneurship along with the ideal of achieving goals and life objectives premised upon the excellence of individual godgifts and talents.[3] It has been reportedly penned in the Amazon blurb of *Democracy in America,*

> In 1831 Alexis de Tocqueville, a young French aristocrat and ambitious civil servant, set out from post-revolutionary France on a journey across America that would take him 9 months and cover 7,000 miles. The result was *Democracy in America,* a subtle and prescient analysis of the life and institutions of 19th-century America. Tocqueville looked to the flourishing democratic system in America as a possible model for post-revolutionary France, believing that the egalitarian ideals it enshrined reflected the spirit of the age and even divine will. His study of the strengths and weaknesses of an evolving democratic society has

> been quoted by every American president since Eisenhower, and remains a key point of reference for any discussion of the American nation or the democratic system.[4]

Thus, the idiom of working alone, akin to John Rambo and attaining greatness and prosperity with the bovine gift of Democracy leaves aside the context of collectivity and the recognized ideal of ameliorating the sins of other nations and principalities before being true to the vocation of being a nation and incentivized hoi polloi. Thus, the Democrats that bedevil the American firmament, (Ideological underpinnings Alas!!!!) also, pinpoint towards the ideal of leading a singular way of policy and life that can have an individual rags-to-riches narrative or an 'Individual John Doe becoming rich and famous' lore. The same ideal of individualism and the go-it-alone approach in the international context earmarks the policy paradigm of the singularly and unilaterally inclined United States of America in an allegedly multipolar world.

In the same manner, Ambassador T P Srinivas writes in the *Hindu* that India and United States have co-terminus aims now after the Paris Climate Change conference as both the nations comprehend and understand the limitations of both the developing world and developed part of the comity of nations. Srinivas writes in the context of the theme of Climate Change, 'U.S. President Donald Trump's accusation against India concerning the Paris Accord that "...the U.S. pays billions of dollars while China, Russia, and India have contributed (to pollution) and will contribute nothing" is inaccurate, misleading and unfair. In fact, India has walked with the U.S. from Stockholm to Paris via Rio de Janeiro, Kyoto and Copenhagen'.[5]

The Ambassador further writes,

> New Delhi has fought for climate justice, equity and fairness all the way, demanding that developing countries should be entitled to maintain and increase their greenhouse gas emissions for survival and developed countries should mandatorily cut their luxury emissions. At the same time, India has also been sensitive to the constraints of the U.S. and the other industrialised nations in reducing emissions.[6]

The question that poses a dilemmatic proposition happens to be that, does the American recalcitrance amounts to a do or die intransigence of intent, purpose or action or the American unilateralist perception in the comity of nations and the American intent is part of the allegation on the go-it-alone approach of the Americans. Even, Tocqueville, years back, went on to describe the American penchant for a well-defined individual streak in the way, Americans handle their homeland, the international firmament and the besieged front.

Coming back to the theme of an alleged American intransigence, one can define the themes and commentaries on the American conflict with the state of Nicaragua. The ICJ found the Americans guilty of illegal and illegitimate interventionism. The ICJ case brief informs us,

> The Court finds it established that, on a date in late 1983 or early 1984, the President of the United States authorized a United States government agency to lay mines in Nicaraguan ports; that in early 1984 mines were laid in or close to the ports of El Bluff, Corinto and Puerto Sandino, either in Nicaraguan internal waters or in its territorial sea or both, by persons in the pay and acting on the instructions of that agency, under the supervision and with the logistic support of United States agents; that neither before the laying of the mines, nor subsequently, did the United States Government issue any public and official warning to international shipping of the existence and location of the mines; and that personal and material injury was caused by the explosion of the mines [...].[7]

The Court chooses a lifeline for the Americans where-in the ICJ holds in its judgement that interventionism should be accounted for and along with that, it must be understood that it was the Contras that were behind the damage caused to the Nicaraguan denomination, and the Americans are not directly responsible for the damage and the carnage in the state of Nicaragua. This is one aspect of the judgement that has received scant interest and attention in the legalese in the international system at large.

One segment of the ICJ judgement also contends,

> In view of the Court, if the provision of 'humanitarian assistance' is to escape condemnation as an intervention in the internal affairs of Nicaragua, not only must it be limited to the purposes hallowed in the practice of the Red Cross, namely 'to prevent and alleviate human suffering', and 'to protect life and health and to ensure respect for the human being'; it must also, and above all, be given without discrimination to all in need in Nicaragua, not merely to the *contras* and their dependants.[8]

Another aspect that goes in favour of the US establishment happens to be that apart from the mines laid out in the territory of the state of Nicaragua, no other major palpable blame can be managed against Washington, and other aspects do pinpoint towards the interventionist approach of the United States. The ICJ judgement holds, 'Except as regards the mines, Nicaragua has not however attributed any breach of humanitarian law to either United States personnel or the "UCLAs" ["Unilaterally Controlled Latino Assets" acronym used by the CIA for Latin American citizens, paid by, and acting under the direct instructions of, United States military or intelligence personnel], as distinct from the *contras*'.[9]

When a war is initiated, a great deal depends upon the practice of psychologically tackling the Government. The call of the hour is that even when only tensions have to be escalated in a subtle or a well-pronounced manner, then the operative idea is that a well-crafted, an assiduously nurtured and spread-out broadsheet of messaging and communication has to be attempted against the adversary. The same allegation was levelled against the United States in the line of duty to harass Nicaragua. The ICJ analysis contended,

> It is also appropriate to recall the circumstances in which the manual of psychological operations was issued. When considering whether the publication of such a manual, encouraging the commission of acts contrary to general principles of humanitarian law, is unlawful, it is material to consider whether that encouragement was offered to persons in circumstances where the commission of such acts was likely or foreseeable.[10]

The ICJ information informs us,

> The Court has however found [...] that at the relevant time those responsible for the issue of the manual were aware of, at the least, allegations that the behaviour of the *contras* in the field was not consistent with humanitarian law; it was in fact even claimed by the CIA that the purpose of the manual was to 'moderate' such behaviour. The publication and dissemination of a manual in fact containing the advice quoted above must therefore be regarded as an encouragement, which was likely to be effective, to commit acts contrary to general principles of international humanitarian law reflected in treaties.[11]

What the Americans did, was, that they published a manual that entailed details about the atrocities being committed by the Nicaraguan government. The manual was part of the American Psychological Operations that aimed at informing the Nicaraguan public about the excesses of the Government in support of the revolting Contras who were being aided and abated by the United States. The Americans published the 'messaging manual' and managed to drop it through aircraft upon the coastal plains in Nicaragua. Some of these manuals were obtained by the Nicaraguan Government and thus emanated the resulting allegation before the ICJ.

All these facets bring us to the grandiloquent Political Contest Model that pits a state actor against the non-state actor. As is well known, the state actor defined by the Government of the day is more accoutred and equipped by the dint of its access to resources. The non-state actor quintessentially, in the *nom de plume* of the understanding, happens to be the terror party actor or the insurgent/separatist that alludes to a spectacular and a publicity-gathering incident in order to get its political cause across to the larger world against a real or imagined slight of the order of repression, violations of humanitarian laws or a theme related to self-determination.[12]

The idea is that this framework is termed as the larger Political Contest Model. This is premised upon the war games and the gladiatorial contests that were historically arranged by the Royalty between charioteers, armoured gladiators and horsemen, all clad in bronze armour in order to entertain the audience gathered in the Roman arcadia or the amphitheatre.[13] In a similar manner, the Contras and the Americans required the all-out Chutzpah of an international but localized conflict in order to bring out the Villainy and the malfeasance of a repressive communist Nicaraguan Regime. It is here as part of the rubric of the Political Contest model that the Americans would be invisible with the Nicaraguan Regime being the repressive, exploitative and the antagonist state actor pitted against the spectacular terror-strivings of the Contras. The interventionist role or a non-role of the United States of America is a different case in point.

If we delve inside the historical details of the Nicaraguan conflict, several interesting details and an attendant narrative develops much in the line of the stereotypical Cold War narrative. A web portal informs us,

> In the 1970s, Anastasio Somoza, Jr., carried human rights abuses to new levels as protests increased following his appropriation of most of the aid for victims of the 1972 Managua earthquake. The Sandinista Front for National Liberation, founded in the '60s, was gaining support among the populace and anyone suspected of giving support to its

> struggle was captured, tortured and often killed. The Carter Administration policy of conditioning military aid on observance of internationally recognized standards of human rights put the Somoza regime into a fury.[14]

It can be further mentioned,

> U.S. troops returned to Nicaragua in the aftermath of Hurricane Mitch in late 1998. Some Nicaraguans, remembering the U.S. military's role in training and arming the contras, opposed their presence. Others, such as the Sandinista farmers and ranchers organization UNAG, worked with them to build schools and clinics. Many observers worry that the troops are part of a deeper game to advance the domination of Central America and its natural resources.

The portal further reports that as part of the extension of the Nicaraguan historical narrative,

> "In 2000, U.S. troops provided medical attention, built two clinics and a school, dug several wells and improved roads and other infrastructure. In 2001, U.S. Ambassador Garza declared that the Nicaraguan military had moved away from its identification with the Sandinistas and now represented "all of Nicaraguan society". Nicaragua, he said, "has taken steps to ... depoliticize its armed forces"'.[15]

Thus, there were attempts at rapprochements with the new understanding reached between the American establishment and the idiom of American intransigence being a creation of the recent origins only. But one factoid remains that American intervention has always been a fact of life in the Nicaraguan case study. All these developments followed the ICJ judgement.

To mull over and culminate the discussion on Central America and the state of Nicaragua, the Americans have always been interventionist in their neighbourhood in continuation of the dictum of Monroe Doctrine. They have been there as a consequence of the competition with the state of Mexico. The American Department of State, Website, informs us the same. The portal contends,

> In the years leading up to the First World War, the United States and Mexican governments competed for political influence in Central America. As a result, the U.S. Government intervened more directly in Nicaraguan affairs in two separate, but related, incidents in 1911 and 1912, with the objective of ensuring the rule of a government friendly

> to U.S. political and commercial interests and preserving political stability in Central America. Although officials within the administration of President William H. Taft saw themselves as intervening to ensure good government, many Nicaraguans became increasingly alarmed at what seemed to be a foreign takeover of their political, banking, and railroad systems.[16]

Thus, despite internal and domestic reservations on the part of a few Nicaraguan interests, the reality of the big brotherly intervention and intrusion remained a part and parcel of the entire ambit of the Central American debate and the extant political scenario. Thus, there is an entire narrative attached to the debate on Nicaragua and United States, where-in the United States has always considered the Latin American terrain as their favourite and rightful backwaters, like the typical water ponds and springs in the Maori lands in the state of New Zealand.

It can be surmised that the United States of America has a few operative clauses to go by as far as the decisions to intervene in the global hot spots is concerned. Various nations and IR observers have pinpointed towards the idea of interests for America to look askance, away from its homeland quarters. Henry Kissinger has written that myriad nations including America intervene due to the involved national interests and also due to the Idealist–Realist schism of spreading democratic ideals, human rights and the ideals of liberty and egalitarianism that happen to be the hallmarks of the American juggernaut of growth, power and pelf-prosperity.

Henry Kissinger and James A Baker III write in one of the articles in the *Washington Post*,

> The change sweeping the Arab world has brought to the forefront a controversy dating to the early days of our Republic. Should American military might be used for idealistic reasons or as an expression of a vital national interest? Or both? Having served four U.S. presidents during a variety of international crises, we view the choice between 'idealism' and 'realism' as a false one. Just as ideals must be applied in concrete circumstances, realism requires context for our nation's values to be meaningful. To separate them risks building policy on sand.[17]

The idealist strain in the American strategic applecart depends upon the ideal of spreading the higher moral perch of America while the Realist strain makes America look around for coalitions and alliances in sync with its national interest and attendant national objectives.

Kissinger and Baker III further write, 'When using force, we must establish a clear and specific goal. The objective of protecting civilians is consistent with our values. But it is inherently difficult to keep such an effort limited. The need for humanitarian intervention almost invariably arises from the necessity of protecting populations from their own governments or from the collapse of government altogether'.[18] Collateral damage is one stick with which the left critiques and other observers of the international humanitarian interventions are known to berate the Americans with. When war occurs and both the sides witness ground action, then civilian casualties as part of military action colours the American objectives that are very much idealist and peacenik in approach and nature.

The authors further write,

> This provides incentives for strategic foreign policy considerations, such as regime change or nation building. But if we articulate a goal of regime change in conjunction with military intervention, we will be expected to employ the means required to effect it. A disconnect risks confusion among allies, adversaries and the American public, as well as mission creep. Failure to achieve proclaimed objectives then turns into a strategic setback.[19]

The striving of the left liberals has been the ideal that all American interventions, with the vanguard being the attrition and mayhem of Vietnam, happen to be the tarnishing blame game with the United States in the context of the American failures at nation building in warring stations such as Iraq. Regime change as an avowed objective cannot be cast as the staple fare excuse for various American interventions, but that is how it is.

In the American parlance, the words and the larger nomenclature, which have been avidly utilized, have been that of Reconstruction and Rehabilitation or, 'Rehab', which amount to an effort by the intervening American interests and the receptacle State's Government that can lead to a lot of strategic, diplomatic and political heartburn for the United States of America. This amplified with the blame game of America-induced collateral damage, akin to the bombardment of the Children Milk Factories in Baghdad during Persian Gulf War I in 1991, leads to the spawning of a bad visage and bad byte for the humanitarian tilt and tenor of the American intervention. Also, there ought to be ample domestic support in the American homeland that needs to be buttressed by a Congressional backing too.The American establishment has to be clear and upfront about its efforts in foreign interventions as they have to be careful that the interventions engaged in, do not germinate a failed state or a nation that has a population militating merely at the name of the United States of America under the palpable appellation of being the 'Great Satan' as the Ayatollahs of West Asia brand the United States of America as! Also, once again the goals and the objectives of the option of the use of force need to be clearly defined if a healthier understanding and a peacenik appellation of America has to be sustained in region-specific positions and globally, too.

Also, a great deal of aspersions has been cast upon the nature of the party actor to the conflict that is being supported by the United States. In a civil war situation, apart from attracting the humanitarian law clauses under the categorizations of IAC and NIAC, the stable visage of America has to be sustained with diligence. An intelligent striving has to be spawned to not let the Mandarins of hate paint the American nation and what all America stands for in a vitriolic colour that makes policy making and further implementation of courageous decisions difficult for the American establishment. In the current context, the yardsticks for American policy can be earmarked in the states such as Syria, Yemen, Iran and Libya, all troubled places in the global polity.

When one refers to all these sustainable concerns in the context of American interventions, then one can cite a study and a report contended by the CNN in October 2015. James Griffiths of CNN World reported about the war in Afghanistan, 'New details are emerging about the deadly U.S. bombing of a Doctors Without Borders hospital in Afghanistan in what the charity has called a "war crime". The commander of U.S. forces there, Gen. John Campbell, said the hospital in the northern city of Kunduz had been struck accidentally after Afghan forces called in air support'.[20] Thus, these American military ministrations have been pointed out by the discerning global community of IR observers and other experts with an intent to highlight the war crime part of the American interventions and war operations in the conflict zones.

Griffiths further writes,

> While the term collateral damage was not as widely used during the Vietnam War as it is in modern conflicts, a statement made to Associated Press journalist Peter Arnett by an unnamed U.S. military official about actions taken against the Viet Cong in Ben Tre city has become iconic in the debate over military action in civilian areas. "It became necessary to destroy the town to save it", the major told Arnett following the

> heavy shelling of the city. Though the validity of the quote has been questioned by some, it is indicative of U.S. strategy at the time. More than 864,000 tons of bombs were dropped during Operation Rolling Thunder alone, compared with 503,000 tons dropped during the entire Pacific Theater of World War II, according to the US Department of Defense.[21]

The Vietnam War and its anthology survives as a genre of the backlash that was aimed at what all was great and grandiloquent about the United States of America. The issue of collateral damage was not very much *au courant* at that point of time, but the needless civilian casualties with their 'large' numbers falsely painted the American military operations in a dark hue of inhuman visage, which was a trail followed by critics in Iraq, Syria and Afghanistan too. It has always been an Asian and South American pet peeve and a fashionable academic exercise to blame the consumption of an expiry medicine also on the American Foreign policy intent. These strains and grains of thought have bedevilled the American tag line in the international polity. Still, President Trump decides aptly that they will not tag along with the actors in the Global Polity and will follow an, "nationalist and Inward looking approach" for the besieged homeland.

Brice Cronin writes in the *Journal of Peace Research*, that, Military organizations that are generally committed to following the laws and customs of war exploit what the author terms 'the collateral damage exemption', by employing legally-sanctioned war-fighting strategies that result in significant numbers of civilian casualties. This exemption shields combatants from legal liability for 'incidental' or 'inadvertent' civilian losses and the destruction of civilian objects that may occur during lawful actions. The author argues that military strategies which promote the use of overwhelming force under conditions that are likely to adversely affect the civilian population on a significant scale and push the boundaries of legal behavior.[22]

Still, the nations that adapt well to the conditionality of the war effort and the recipient nation, are able to mitigate and decrease the violence and losses in the civilian context. The deliberate attacks on civilian constellations must be eschewed all together akin to My Lai in the heady conflict zone of Vietnam in the sixties. The military acts that are indefensible must be avoided by the American establishment but still when the terror mongers are difficult to sift in the twilight zone stage of mixed-up demographics and terrain, the nations such as the United States and even nationalities such as India are left with no other feasible option, but, to battle the human shields such as in the Indian state of Jammu and Kashmir and now Pulwama in PoK.

One can take a brief look at the NATO strike force conditionality in the case of the State of Libya. One Amnesty International report suggests the nature of the UNSC 1973 and militates against the NATO strikes in Libya in 2011. The report runs as,

> On 19 March 2011 several member states of the North Atlantic Treaty Organization (NATO), including the USA, the UK and France, launched a military campaign with air and naval strikes against Colonel Mu'ammar al-Gaddafi's forces. The strikes were launched pursuant to UN Security Council (UNSC) resolution 1973 (2011) of 17 March 2011, which authorized member states "to take all necessary measures (...) to protect civilians and civilian populated areas under threat of attack in the Libyan Arab Jamahiriya" and introduced a "no fly zone" above Libya'.[23]

What fails to strike is the presence of the clause against collateral damage and war crimes that must not be committed during the war or the ongoing conflict. The irony of the civil war in Libya was that the American and the rebel dominance of the total air space in the State of Libya was not found to be enough to avoid the scourge of 'Collateral Damage' in Libya, once, the Gaddafi's forces had capitulated largely.

Organizations such as Amnesty International have been largely critical of the various American interventions. The same Amnesty International report contends,

> NATO's military actions in Libya had to comply with the rules of international humanitarian law (IHL) applicable in international armed conflict.25 IHL contains the rules and principles that seek to protect anyone who is not directly participating in hostilities: notably civilians and anyone, including those who were previously participating in hostilities, who are wounded, have surrendered or been captured, or otherwise incapacitated. It sets out standards of humane conduct and limits the means and methods of conducting military operations. Its central purpose is to limit, to the extent feasible, human suffering in times of armed conflict.[24]

The report further narrates,

> The four Geneva Conventions of 1949 and their two Additional Protocols of 1977 are among the principal IHL instruments. Many of the specific rules included in these treaties form part of customary IHL and are thus binding on all parties to any type of armed conflict, including on armed groups. Violations of many of these rules can constitute war crimes.[25]

All the principles and rules cited in this briefing are part of customary international law and are binding on all parties to an armed conflict. The following fundamental principles of IHL (which have been codified in Protocol I of 1977 as specific rules governing the conduct of hostilities) appear particularly relevant for assessing the civilian casualties caused by NATO strikes, namely[26]: (1) The principle of distinction requires that the parties to a conflict 'shall at all times distinguish between the civilian population and combatants and between civilian objects and military objectives and accordingly shall direct their operations only against military objectives'.[27] Article 51(2) spells out unambiguously that the 'civilian population as such as well as individual civilians, shall not be the object of attack'. In addition to direct attacks on civilians, IHL also prohibits indiscriminate attacks, which are those 'of a nature to strike military objectives and civilians or civilian objects without distinctions'.[28]

Article 57(2) of Protocol I specifies necessary precautions including everything feasible must be done to verify that targets are military objectives; means and methods of attack must be selected with a view to minimizing harm to civilians and civilian objects.[29] The proportionality of a planned attack must be assessed; an attack must be cancelled or suspended if it becomes apparent it is wrongly directed or disproportionate, and effective advance warning must be given of attacks that may affect the civilian population, unless circumstances do not permit. Where it is unclear whether an object is used for military purposes, 'it shall be presumed not to be so used'.[30] Still the issue is that these paraphernalia are good enough for the usage of a military or a diplomatic manual but the only ideal which can be practically utilized is that of 'It shall be presumed not to be so used', which is a maxim that does not place the doubt on the head of the interventionist state, which, the United States of America happens to be on more than one occasion.

Also, it needs to be kept in the reckoning that all the modalities mentioned in the Geneva Conventions and the protocols are difficult to be practicalized in reality on ground zero. The heat and the grime of war along with mechanized forces with the Americans having the telecommunication and technological advantages, too play a role in the nature of violence and damages caused during warfare. Still, the ides of the grime and heat of the conflict preclude a verbatim adherence to the conditions and protocoled itinerary. It is not practically feasible for even the most "humanist" of forces and defence personnel in training, tradition, values, sentiment and brio, to order around the 'Rangroots' to clinically adhere to the conditions of International Humanitarian Law, when the non-state adversary too seeks leverage through illicit and illegitimate means and enjoins and enjoys a 'homestead advantage'. The Pulwama massacre by Islamabad and the Indian Riposte in PoK is a great example of how New Delhi clinically avoided collateral damage in its Mirage-2000 attacks.

NOTES

1. *Military and Paramilitary Activities in and Against Nicaragua* (*Nicaragua v. United States of America*), Judgment, 27 June 1986. http://www.icj-cij.org/docket/?sum=367&p1=3&p2=3&case=70&p3=5.
2. Ibid.
3. Tocqueville, Alexis De, *Democracy in America*, London: Penguin Classics, 2003, pp. 12–20.
4. Tocqueville, *Democracy in America*.
5. Sreenivasan, T.P., 'Cool Down the Rhetoric', *The Hindu*, 23 May 2017.
6. Ibid.
7. International Court of Justice, *Case Concerning Military and Paramilitary Activities In and Against Nicaragua*. https://casebook.icrc.org/case-study/icj-nicaragua-v-united-states. Accessed 22 May 2017.
8. Ibid.
9. Ibid.
10. Ibid.
11. Ibid.
12. Gadi Wolsfeld, 'Chapter Five: The Political Contest Model', in *News, Public Relations and Power*, Simon Cottle (ed.), London: Sage Publications, 1992.
13. Ibid.
14. 'Background on US Military Involvement in Nicaragua'. http://www.soaw.org/index.php?option=com_content&view=article&id=325. Accessed 28 May 2017.
15. Ibid.
16. United States Department of State Archives, 'US Intervention in Nicaragua', 1911/1912. https://2001-2009.state.gov/r/pa/ho/time/ip/108629.htm. Accessed 22 May 2017.
17. Kissinger, Henry, James A. Baker III, 'Grounds for US Military Interventions', *Washington Post*, 8 April 2011.
18. Ibid.
19. Ibid.

20. Griffins, James. 'Collateral Damage: A Brief History of US Mistakes at War'. http://edition.cnn.com/2015/10/06/middleeast/us-collateral-damage-history/. Accessed 10 May 2017.
21. Ibid.
22. Cronin, Bruce, 'Reckless Endangerment Warfare: Civilian Casualties and the Collateral Damage Exception in International Humanitarian Law', *Journal of Peace Research*, 12 February 2013.
23. Amnesty International, 'Libya: The Forgotten Victims of NATO Strikes', Amnesty International Publication, 2012.
24. Ibid.
25. Ibid.
26. For further details and referencing of applicable IHL rules, see Amnesty International, 'The Battle for Libya: Killings, Disappearances and Torture', 13 September 2011, pp. 27–30. www.amnesty.org/en/library/info/MDE19/025/2011/en.
27. Article 48, Protocol I, Geneva Conventions Text.
28. Article 51(4), Geneva Conventions Text.
29. Article 52(1) of the 1977 Additional Protocol I (Protocol Additional to the Geneva Conventions of 12 August 1949, and relating to the Protection of Victims of International Armed Conflicts, Protocol I, 8 June 1977) defines civilian objects as 'all objects which are not military objectives'.
30. Article 52(3), Protocol I, Geneva Conventions Text.

7

Mama San in the East: The Vietnam Syndrome

VIETNAM War and the mention of the South East Asian nation, too, prepares the American establishment for what all has gone wrong for the American nation, as US leads the rest of the world polity with its tenet of Manifest Destiny. Vietnam was a parallel development with the idea that anti-war protests and the flower children movement have been treated as an epochal event in the souring of the American Dream. The American Dream happens to be the celebration of the American entrepreneurship ideal of hard work, respect for human labour and a belief in the individual comprehension of mankind. Vietnam was a test case for the American establishment, where-in the American self-belief in its invulnerability and pelf of power and military girth was shaken to no bounds by the ragtag bunch of Chippenueks, the rebels of the Viet Cong forces led by Ho Chi Minh. Several American mainstream movies such as Platoon, Born on the Fourth of July along with Rambo have done justice to the crisis of credibility that had been faced by the American establishment in the turbulent sixties which was overtly played up by national dailies such as *New York Times* and *Washington Post*. The Steven Speilberg flick, "The Post" beatifically brings out the tug of war between the White House and the Fourth Eastate as the fervent frenzy in the house of Katherine Graham is reflected by the endless reams of Pentagon Papers which besmirch the American establishment as part of the epochal movie's narrative.

It was a defeat that was indigestible and intolerably insane for a roiled and troubled American establishment and the entire societal psyche of the American homeland. It took another two decades in the aftermath of Persian Gulf War I, that the American warring establishment could elude and emerge massively scathed out of the debacle in Vietnam after the 'New World Order' speech of President George Bush, Sr, which proclaimed the End of Days as written and profoundly propagated by Francis Fukuyama. Thus, the go-it-alone approach of the United States was validated by the American dismemberment of Saddam Hussein's war machine, which failed to live up to its name and emerged as rickety and belonging to a World War II variant. The unilateralist streak of the dirty war, as the Vietnam War is known as, attempted to be festooned upon the South East Asian nation that was validated with a military victory in the decade of the sixties and seventies. But, the commilstrain had to be "contained".

Vietnam was referred to as a 'Cesspool', a 'vortex of mutilation' by the American observers after witnessing the violence and perdition in the badlands of Vietnam. Similarly, General Westmoreland contended in a personal interview after the war had ended, "The Chippenhueks would climb the trees and ferries and disappear into the night. The Mama San who cleaned the Utensils and swept the floor would soon disappear into the night trails and leap from the six feet grass belts to harass the American GI's'. Thus, the scenario in the Vietnam War is that of a cesspool of violence and anarchy, which tested the best of the American men, who were younglings and were fighting miles away in the strange and inhospitable tropical warfronts.

The coterminous social and political development that was occurring in the American Domestic scene, deserves a mention too. It was the much anointed, lorewise, the anti-war movement that amalgamated with the spirit of University protests and left-wing and liberal activism in the form of the hippy culture that was finding a way through the race angst in the American homeland, too. It was not the Lyndon B Johnson's 'Great Society' that fired the imagination of the American popular myth and lore along with the larger public psyche in the United State of America. What was the need of the hour was the Tennessee Valley Project's high public spirit that was the pet peeve of the 'new deal' as was envisioned by President Franklin Delano Roosevelt. 'Was Vietnam tenable?' is the question that can be asked going by the International Law of Intervention. But, we should not forget that the war was in US's national interest in tandem with containment.

The position of the United States as to whether there is a dispute endangering international peace or security is ambivalent.[1] Brian K Landsberg blames the entire charge on the United States of America as being the flouter of International Law. He writes,

> Vietnam is presently the site of armed conflict between guerrillas and the Diem government. It is clear that the guerrillas have the support of North Vietnam, and that the United States supports Diem. The East-West controversy over Vietnam has brought forth charges by each side that the other has been breaching promises made at Geneva in 1954 and otherwise violating international law.[2]

Apparently, Secretary of State, Dean Rusk has labelled the Viet Cong activities 'a threat to the peace',[3] and has said that 'the stakes are greater than South Vietnam itself'.[4] These statements are in accord with the US Declaration on Indo-China made at the close of the 1954 Geneva Conference: 'The United States would view any renewal of the aggression in violation of the aforesaid agreements with grave concern and as seriously threatening international peace and security'.[5] The State Department says that 'The present balance of forces between independent and Communist states in Asia, would be tipped perilously if Viet-Nam, Cambodia, and Laos fell under Communist domination. What then would be the prospects for Thailand and Burma, for Pakistan and India, for Malaya and Indonesia'?[6] Thus, it all amounted to the American policy paradigm of containment of the Communist States and security interests in the South East Asia. Herein, it was contended that if the Dominoes of Vietnam, Laos and Cambodia would fail, then, the American national and global interests in the context of stemming the flow and the expanse of communism, would have fallen by the wayside.

The *New York Times* reports that the US officials discount 'the danger of early involvement or foreign Communist and United States troops in direct combat...'.[7] These apparent contradictions in American statements are probably caused by a desire to reassure.

South Vietnam and the build up of the American and world sentiment against the North Vietnamese, and the conflicting desire to justify keeping the Vietnamese question out of the United Nations.[8] It should finally be noted that the Soviet Union,[9] Communist China, and, according to the *New York Times*, 'some Western allies',[10] all claimed that the dispute was dangerous. The chances were such that despite the American military advantage and the home advantage to the Viet Cong guerrillas, the threat to peace was accentuated as the war could have spilled onto China and, thus, an Armageddon would have been on the cards. The Cold War credentials were definitively finding a place in the US–Vietnam narrative that was a classical and stereotypical instance of a standard cold war conflict.

It does not appear that the sole source of the Diem government's trouble was Viet Minh intervention. President Kennedy impliedly recognized that some of the guerrilla forces were Vietnamese when he said, 'There has been evidence that *some* of these forces have come from beyond the borders'.[11] A Rand Corporation researcher found that whole areas of the country were friendly to the Communists, but were actively hostile to the Diem regime.[12] Vietnamese intelligence reports say that 20 per cent of the villagers of the nation favour the Viet Cong. Thus, we must credit the conclusion that Vietnam is engaged in 'a political and social revolution which, for all of the outside Communist interference, has deep, indigenous, popular roots'.[13] Thus, the Americans were fatigued due to the homeland advantage of the Viet Minh forces. The Viet Minh, given the advantage of the local terrain and the language along with the ethnic similarities, always had the upper hand though, what later on went on to be called as 'Shock and Awe' affronts at the American interests.

The Sheer American War Purpose in Self-Defence and International Law

The various International Law perspectives have to be taken into consideration if the *nom de plume* of what went on in the Vietnam War has to be understood. But, the tenets of International Law can be read both ways, where-in the idea of people facing a despot has to be delved inside with incisive analysis. A harassed population has a right to freedom and a life devoid of penury, and fixated on the side of the fence is the notion that any external actor such as the United States is not to be alleged if it comes to the rescue of a beleaguered nation such as the challenged population of Vietnam. Benjamin B Ferencz contends,

> The legal right of any lawful government to defend itself against violent overthrow can hardly be questioned. The right of any government to join in the defense of its allies or friends to protect their or its own vital interests, is an ancient and well established practice. It is, however, also

> part of the American heritage that the people, feeling themselves aggrieved by a foreign power or a tyrannical regime, have the legal right and 'it is their duty to throw off such government'. The United States has the legal right to assist in the defense of the government of South Vietnam.[14]

According to Richard Falk, 'If the US Government had abided by international law, the dreadful experience of the Vietnam War would not have occurred'.[15] Falk's perception might be too early to declare the American decision to go beyond the supply of military advice and suggestions to the Diem Government. As it can be witnessed that in the liberal conception of America's South Vietnamese policy, the United States is not prevented from aiding any allied democracy in the truest conception of collective security and cooperation in a peace regime far the larger international system.

There is an international jurisprudence that is present in the role playing by the supreme judiciary of America. Much in line with the cause of international law, a couple of cases were contested in the US Supreme Court that reflected the churn of the domestic population in America. Apart from it all, the Supreme Court too dithered in declaring the United States of America as an out-and-out aggressor nation state. Also, the mandate of the American executive was largely not questioned by the US Supreme Court in which the Court found the American Political establishment capable enough to go ahead with the tackling of any crisis and strife in the larger international system. Anyway, the President of the United States is considered to be the whole and sole personage who acts as the Supreme commander of the American forces and can come out with an executive decision to declare war on any nation state, which turns rogue.

In a few of the Supreme Court cases in the United States, the debate and the face-saving rationale for any act by the US government have been reflected well. In *United States v. Sisson*, a federal judge dismissed a challenge to the Vietnam War's constitutionality because it involved 'just the sort of evidence, policy considerations, and constitutional principles which elude the normal processes of the judiciary and which are far more suitable for determination by coordinate branches of the government'. In *Sarnoff v. Shultz*, the US Ninth Circuit Court ruled on, and the US Supreme Court was petitioned to reconsider, the constitutionality of the then Treasury Secretary, George Schultz, allocating funds to the Vietnam War in spite of the fact that an official Declaration of War had never been made.

The Supreme Court voted 6-3 to not reconsider the lower court's ruling, thus, upholding Ninth Circuit's ruling that George Shultz had been tacitly authorized by the US Congress to allocate funds to the Vietnam War by virtue of Congress's approval of the federal budgets that included these war funds.[16] The entire decision to intervene in Vietnam by the United States cannot be broken down into micro-segments on the lines of a political and procedural debate as to which part of the executive gave the go ahead while which other part of the executive went ahead with the executioners' task of going ahead with the war. The separation of powers is in itself a segment and a key pillar of the American political system that can be attacked but not gainfully vilified. Though no formal declaration of war was ever made in the American context, it can be argued that when the American vessels of the order of Turner Jay and another vessel named, Maddox, were attacked by the Viet Cong in the Gulf of Tonkin, then, at that point of time, a war rationale was reached by President Johnson and later on the war was continued to a certain extent by President Nixon. Also, the war rationale was a retaliatory reaction by the American side though earlier skirmishes with the VC could have ignited the military action from the Americans much earlier in the day. Chapter VII of the Vietnam War prohibits war that is not meant to sustain peace and sustainability of the world peace in accordance with Article 42 of the UN Charter, but the UN Charter also gives a partial clean chit to war in accordance with Article 51 that postulates about a war fought in self-defence. Also, going by the US Law, the conflict in Vietnam was not illegal or illicit, but it led to the idiom of even the domestic population blaming the American establishment for the war effort in the 'Dirty War'.

The web portal of the CNN brings out five lesser known facts about the Vietnam War. The CNN report contends,

(1) "When the choices were Vietnam, jail or draft-dodging by going to Canada, some young men panicked and devised ways to fail the military's physical exam, including mutilating themselves, starving or pretending to be gay. The compulsory draft, which had been initiated during World War II, meant registration for young men was mandatory at 18.

(2) As casualties rose, country's flower children segments and the University youths increasingly turned against the war. The official line was that Americans were winning in Vietnam, but the evening news told a

different story. 'What Vietnam did to America via television was to introduce us to a new kind of America', said author Lawrence Wright. 'One that was not pure, one that committed the same kinds of atrocities that are always committed in war, but, we had never allowed ourselves to see them'.[17]

(3) By the early 1960s, South Vietnam's conventionally trained army was no match for the Vietcong's guerrilla-style tactics. In addition, South Vietnam's Buddhist majority revolted against their President, Ngo Dinh Diem. They saw the Catholic ruler as a tyrant. The Western-educated Diem, however, wielded absolute power and rose to the keel of a dictator by the summer of 1963. The CIA discussed toppling the regime. With US knowledge, Diem was killed by South Vietnamese Gnerals on 2 November 1963. Kennedy immediately regretted Diem's death and US support for the coup.[18]

(4) In the late 1950s, during the Eisenhower administration, Vietnam had split into North Vietnam, which was communist, and South Vietnam which was supported by the United States of America. Cold War anxieties dictated that if the North Vietnamese communists prevailed, the rest of Southeast Asia would fall like dominoes. When President Kennedy took office in 1961, he vowed not to allow South Vietnam to fall to communism.[19] Thus, akin to every nation and its historical and nationalist myth and lore, the various nations have been addicted to a nationally controversial conspiracy theory and some factoids that pepper the narrative of a war. Akin to that, television coverage brought the war right to the drawing rooms of the American denizens for the first time in American contemporary history. In a manner, the Americans were asked to explain the violence and rationale behind the military draft and the decision to sacrifice young patriotic Americans in far-off hostile lands. The crux is that nations have a hallowed trail of select myths and lore attached to their narrative and such small meta-narratives congeal into a larger narrative for the United States akin to other nations in the larger international system. All in all, the American error did not lie in the executive decision's alleged illegality to go to war with North Vietnam.

Despite everything, Vietnam War finds a place in the pantheon of the American wars, conflicts and interventions. It would be an oversimplification to posit that the United States played the role of a neo-imperialist power along with being a global hegemon. In the light of the issues of cold war and the staid rivalry with Soviet Union, America was left with no other option but to intervene in the Vietnam War in order to sustain its own national interest–oriented priorities in the larger international system. The question that emerges as a pertinent one and is a real rankling factor with the global audiences and the other observers of American interventions is 'why exactly did the United States intervene in the war in South East Asia'? The United States, primarily did not want any other nation to get involved with the region and did not want a strategically pivot state to fall as part of the expansionist strategy of the cold war rival, Soviet Union.

The Quora portal can be cited to glean historical facts concerning the hallowed and controversial tenets of the Vietnam War. It can be construed that historically Laos, Cambodia and Vietnam formed the corpus of the region of 'Indo-China' that changed hands from the French to the Germans all the way to the Japanese dominion and back to the French domination to be referred to as 'French Indo-China'. The Quora portal informs,

> Vietnam, Laos and Cambodia had been combined into a French colony called 'French Indochina' back in 1887. However, in 1940, the French government fell and was replaced with a German puppet government. The Japanese saw an opportunity and in September of 1940, invaded and occupied French Indochina. This occupation would continue until 1945, at which point the French attempted to re-establish their hold on Indochina. This went badly for the French. The Viet Minh (the League for the Independence of Vietnam) had spent four years fighting the Japanese for independence—with US and Chinese support—and weren't about to settle for French colonial status. By 1946, Indochina was in a state of war.[20]

Thus, akin to a few other conflict zones of the Global polity, Indo-China was too tarred and made turbulent by the vituperations and the operations of a regional conflict that soon witnessed the involvement of cold war rivals.

The Pentagon Papers Pandemonium

The general idea that the author follows and attempts to eke out rather blandly is that Vietnam War and its attendant myth should not be treated as a Plain Jane conspiracy theorization. It will be an oversimplification to contend that documents such as the Draft Pentagon Papers exposed the United States of America for the so-called carnage and vicious collateral damage that they unleashed on the unsuspecting Vietnamese population. This kind of an allegation does not hold much water as the United States too suffered massive losses and casualties in the conflict that ensued during the raging Vietnam War and its times. The question that rises is 'what are the nature and content of the Pentagon Papers'? The National Archives informs us,

> The Pentagon Papers, officially titled 'Report of the Office of the Secretary of Defense Vietnam Task Force', was commissioned by Secretary of Defense Robert McNamara in 1967. In June of 1971, small portions of the report were leaked to the press and widely distributed. However, the publications of the report that resulted from these leaks were incomplete and suffered from many quality issues.[21]

Thus, the various publications and sections of the Fourth Estate, which shed a great deal of vitriolic ink upon the American planning, intent, the nature of military and advisory opinions in Vietnam, created a sort of conspiratorial air about the fundamentals of US Foreign Policy and its intent about international military and diplomatic interventions. It is through this clarificatory exercise that the American involvement in the Vietnam War ought to be dealt through with gumption, academic alacrity with honesty.

The Pentagon Papers, too, provide a large textual narrative of the entire history of the American involvement in the Vietnam War along with positing the entire counterinsurgency narrative and efforts of the American establishment along with tracing the trajectory of the US war planning, strategy and activities and ops, as they developed in the face of stiff resistance from the North Vietnamese region. These much vaunted documents were initially internal documents that bore largely on the policy making along with being classified material that were originally meant for internal circulation, but, were later on released as public releases apart from being part of the higher Governmental Departments.

One can cite the strategic reading from the Pentagon Papers. One of the studies by General Lansdale can be referred to here:

> General Lansdale reports on his January visit to Vietnam: 'The U.S. should recognize that Vietnam is in a critical condition and should treat it as a combat area of the cold war'. He recommends strong support for Diem personally as the best available South Vietnamese leader, and

> the prompt transfer of Ambassador Durbrow, whose relations with Diem are poor.[22]

The author will utilize further references from the principal text of Pentagon Papers to subscribe to the arguments and the original American standpoint in the context of the details, rationale and the public opinion aspect of the conflict. The Pentagon Papers are considered to be the grand expose on the American establishment but that is another canard to beat black and blue, the American nation, its people and its larger establishment along with its all pervading Dream. Without looking at the niceties of chronology, one can delve inside the rubric of the Geneva Accords that go a long way in advancing both the American and the counter-American argument.

The document cited as the US Military Planning and Diplomatic Maneuver, 1954, leads us on to a better understanding of the charges that have been labelled against the United States of America. As an instance, it is alleged that the United States of America attempted to move ahead with the scuttling of the Geneva Accords or any other agreement on Indo-China. The citation of the Pentagon Papers refutes that charge.

It contends,

> It is charged that the U.S. tried to sabotage the Geneva Conference, first by manoeuvring to prevent the conference from taking place, then by attempting to subvert a settlement, and finally, by refusing to guarantee the resulting agreements of the conference. The documentation on this charge is complete, but by no means unambiguous. While 'sabotage' may be a strong word, it is evident that the U.S. by its actions and statements during this period did seek to down-play the conference, disassociate itself from the results, and thereby did cast doubt on the stability of the accords.[23]

Sabotage might be a strong term that militates against the vagaries of conflict but still America was not all in the alleged seat of attempting to scuttle the Geneva Accords.

The Pentagon Papers inform us that the American aggressiveness was on the rise and an upswing with the American stress on no hand holding with the communists becoming the cynosure of all attention. It is mentioned in the segment titled as 'The Pentagon Papers: the Geneva Accords',

> This rebel-led emphasis on a military approach put in the context of - that Washington referred to as 'united action', of the same character as

> UN intervention in Korea—broad, multilateral, and military. Even as the French-Vietnamese military position continued to deteriorate on the battlefield, the U.S. became more convinced than ever of the need for decisive military victory. The recent experience of Korea only served to convince Washington that meaningful compromise with the communists was impossible.[24]

The fundamental premise of the Containment doctrine was that the annulment of the strain of communism in the affected states was the call of the day. America did not preferably vouch for a compromise.

The same document informs that the United States intended to spawn a regional buttressing for the region, where-in the Americans would go all the way gung ho and replete with brio against the expansiveness and the infectiously insidious spread of the Soviet Union–led communist tirade and "minaretism" of the Russian nation. Apart from attempting to create a regional Anti-Comintern, the American establishment intended to keep alive the tenet of American interventionism, too, that would allow the idiom of the 'American presence' intact in South East Asia. The section on Geneva Accords can be cited verbatim, 'As the negotiations at the conference progressed, Washington shifted. Its weight moved from intervention through united action and instead concentrated on unifying the West into a regional military pact and creating a united diplomatic front at the conference to obtain the best possible settlement for the West. The implied threat of U.S. intervention, however, was allowed to remain'.[25] Thus, America kept open the twin channels before itself. One being the spawning of a regional anti-communist pact to conjoin the regional states in the rigmarole of a regional stronghold and an embankment against the Communist flow and the surge.The other one being the preventive canard of unilateralist American military action and a surge much on the lines of what the United States attempted in the aftermath of the initial military action, in the state of Iraq.

The United States of America has been targeted incriminatingly in a repeated manner as part of a strategy to brand the grandiloquent nation as a unilateralist and arm-twisting hegemon, which is a rather fashionable tea party drawing room collective-speak, ministration and tame palaver of the communists down the south of the Globe. Salvatore Babones writes from the fence of the critics who contend that is the US hegemony here to stay?[26] The literature from the fence of the critics of America might be in abundance, but the cold start manner in which they outrightly castigate the United States reflects an 'International Relations pogrom' that militates against and does irreparable damage not only to the sturdiness and the tangible girth of America, but to the popular travails of the United States in the general imagination of the global polity. Babones castigates America on the popular and internationally fashionable count of being a unilateralist and a forceful arm-twister and a go-it-alone nation with preponderance of power and economic heft. He writes in the *National Interest,*

> "The idea of American hegemony is as old as Benjamin Franklin, but has its practical roots in World War II. The United States emerged from that war as the dominant economic, political and technological power. The only major combatant to avoid serious damage to its infrastructure, its housing stock or its demographic profile, the United States ended the war with the greatest naval order of battle ever seen in the history of the world. It became the postwar home of the United Nations, the International Monetary Fund and the World Bank. And, of course, the United States had the bomb. America was, in every sense of the word, a hegemon."[27]

Thus, the preponderance of America is not only what a Fukuyama or a Fareed Zakaria would talk about, but it's a finality going by 'the supreme statistics', SS, of the American juggernaut that might get shaken by the global vicissitudes of power sways and economic cycles, but the writ large crests of the Empire, are, here to stay. America can subsist comfortably in the role of a leveller and a regulator nation state with the mythical buttressing of a non-hegemonic mantle and halo.

Babones further writes,

> Hegemony is a word used by social scientists to describe leadership within a system of competing states. The Greek historian Thucydides used the term to characterize the position of Athens in the Greek world in the middle of the fifth century BC. Athens had the greatest fleet in the Mediterranean; it was the home of Socrates and Plato, Sophocles and Aeschylus; it crowned its central Acropolis with the solid-marble temple to Athena known to history as the Parthenon. Athens had a powerful rival in Sparta, but no one doubted that Athens was the hegemon of the time until Sparta defeated it in a bitter twenty-seven-year war.[28]

Thus, it is my perception of a question of leadership that makes one mull over the larger questions and ponderables of who dictates and why does the rest of the international system relegate the other powers to the backburner. America provides sheer leadership. The domination it generates is not hegemony, but a functional attribute and a functional consequence of the 'workings' of power and economic pelf. In a way, the world system leads through a balancer and a Joker player as Morton Kaplan would have it that acts as a mediator nation. Some of the players in the international system are bound to have a grouse with the leader, but, the larger comity falls in line. It is not even a falling in line, but, an international cooperative paradigm that seeks to congeal the larger international system in one singular, peaceful and harmonious whole, despite academic and other reservations as to the entire 'role playing' and "game-seeking behaviour" by a much vilified United States of America and its existential rationale.

The stakes of American hegemony are much higher and significantly poised in the true constraints of the international system. In my perception, if the American order suffers, then the rest of the international order suffers with it, akin to a gradual rot and not as an avalanche. Robert Kagan writes similarly in the February 2012 edition of the *New Republic* as quoted in the *Economist,*

> The present world order—characterized by an unprecedented number of democratic nations; a greater global prosperity, even with the current crisis, than the world has ever known; and a long peace among great powers—reflects American principles and preferences, and was built and preserved by American power in all its political, economic, and military dimensions. If American power declines, this world order will decline with it. It will be replaced by some other kind of order, reflecting the desires and the qualities of other world powers. Or perhaps it will simply collapse, as the European world order collapsed in the first half of the twentieth century. The belief, held by many, that even with diminished American power 'the underlying foundations of the liberal international order will survive and thrive', as the political scientist G. John Ikenberry has argued, is a pleasant illusion.[29]

It is this pleasant surprise and a serendipity that reflects the unnerving preponderance of America with the undeniable foundations of the global international order in line with the tedium of 'Leadership'. America went all the way in a way to lead the liberal order's standpoint and positioning in the creaky and wet tropics of Vietnam. They wanted a leader to take over the anarchic mist in the badlands of Vietnam—once again an American perspective.

In psychological terms, there is a much accepted idiom of leadership competencies. America is destined to rule the roost and lead the global firmament in the Manifest Destiny argument. The National Security Strategy of 2017 unveiled by the American President argues for the idea that India can become the Global leader in countering all state and non state actor threats in the future of times. It is a success of PM Modi's Diplomacy that the partnership with United States is morphing into a true-blue allyhood. Which is the other psychobabble argument? It follows something like this. The first indicator is the *nom de plume* of Social Intelligence. Ronald Riggio writes in *Leadership Today*, 'Social intelligence is quite broad, but can best be seen in terms of understanding of social situations and dynamics, and the ability to operate effectively in a variety of social situations. Our research suggests that social intelligence, which we define as a constellation of social performance, sensitivity to social situations, and role-playing skill are critically important for effective leadership'.[30] He points out five indicators of leadership that is an innate quality in any working sphere all the way to the diplomatic sphere of IR. Vietnam and the larger Indo-China could have been stabilized with a leader-nation which could have been the United States of America. Thus, the Asiatic space too bespeaks of a vacuum that needs to be filled in by an International Supervisor and a Corporate Mandarin, where-in new and fresh outcomes are the order of the day.

The author further writes, 'A complement to social intelligence, emotional intelligence is our ability to communicate at the emotional level, understand emotions and emotional situations, and be in tune with our own emotions. These are particularly related to the leadership of "charisma"'.[31] Thus, going all the way back to the Weberian context of leadership, the entire conception of leadership is a global issue and a true international context. The point that can be raised in the context of the Viet Cong–inflicted war is that being emotionally responsive to the 'other and the antagonist' is not a part of the mandate of a fighting force, but, socialization is definitively a consequence of international conflict.

Thus, being a leader in a parched and fissiparously violent and turbulent order, such as in Indo-China, is an offshoot of the liberal thought. Another regular attribute of the entire theme of global leadership happens to be prudence. Aristotle writes in his work, *Nicomachean Ethics: Book Six*,

> Those whom we call prudent, deliberate well about what is good and advantageous to themselves and about life as a whole. One doesn't deliberate about things, which are unchanging or which are not in one's power to do. Therefore prudence can't be scientific knowledge or an art. Prudence is a disposition with true reason and ability for actions concerning human goods. The word for temperance is derived from the word for prudence in the Greek civilizational syntax. Prudence is the virtue of that part of the soul which can form opinions.[32]

It is true reason of nation interest that the American establishment and the thought pattern utilized for itself in its myriad interventions in the international system—the nation state with the conflictual hot-bed of Vietnam, being, a singular case in point.

There is no dearth of literature on the supporters of America's national interest argument. Renowned journals such as the *Economist, Huffington Post* and *National Interest,* have written biblically about the rigmarole of American interventions and the attendant debates and deliberations. It would be interesting to note the aftermath of the Vietnam War after the storm over the 'Rightness' of the American objectives has settled down. David Duong, a Vietnamese boat child writes evocatively about the American intervention in Vietnam and the role played by all pervasiveness and the timelessness of the expanse of the American dream and the attendant culture.

Duong writes,

> It is has been 40 years since the ending of the Vietnam War when the last American helicopter left from the rooftops of Saigon; 40 years since my father, a solider for the Republic of Vietnam, was sent to re-education camp, where he was confined for seven years of hard labor for his crimes of 'siding' with the Americans. It has been 40 years since over 2 million people fled Vietnam via sea and land, seeking freedom from communism —a journey where it is estimated by the United Nations High Commissioner for Refugees that up to 400,000 perished.[33]

He further writes,

> I was 5 years old when I left Vietnam with my parents, after my father's release from re-education camp. My initial memories of America include my mother explaining to me when we tried our first slice of cheese pizza that this was the American version of a French crepe. I also remember that my father rode a donated bicycle to his first day of work, proudly wearing the tailored suit he brought from Vietnam

> because he remembered from American movies that everyone wore suits to work.[34]

On 30 April, the annual conglomeration of Vietnamese diaspora gets together with the idea of Reunification Day while donning black suits in order to ruminate over what all was lost and what kind of land was lost to violence, war and the attendant perdition. The entire gamut of the Vietnam War divides the experience of the Vietnamese denizens in a pre-75 and a post-75 furlough that initially bears the painful memories of boat people and the nationwide food shortages and the communist re-education camp as an aftermath of the Vietnam War. Critics such as Thomas Donnelly mark the epicentre of the debate that militates against the national interest and the objectives argument of America. Donnelly writes on the American Enterprise Institute web portal,

> Hillary was in full apology mode when asked to explain her 2003 vote to authorize the invasion of Iraq: 'From my perspective, it was my mistake'. And she quickly went on to assert, 'We are not putting ground troops in to Iraq ever again, and we're not putting troops into Syria'. At the moment, there are more 5,000 U.S. troops in Iraq, and with operations to retake Mosul looming, the Obama Administration has announced plans to send another 500. The deployment includes a hefty portion of commandos and teams of advisers with Iraqi army battalions; they are most definitely 'on the ground'. This is double-talk that Lyndon Johnson would approve.[35]

Akin to Vietnam, an attendant myth and lore has developed in the context of the American intervention in Iraq, too. The idea is that the American Democrat, Hillary Clinton was also a part of the group of senators to give a go-ahead to the Iraq War. Akin to it, like some of the Congressmen live in the war guilt of Vietnam, some of the Democrats run the gamut of war guilt in the context of Iraq too.

The American Dream too entailed global trotting and interventionism once the American Dream had run over the "Entangling Alliances" argument. Christian G Appy writes,

> I did not know that there was a bad war. George Evans grew up in Pitsburgh and staring [*sic*] at an age of six years, he helped his father deliver blocks of ice to the poverty stricken and working class people who could not afford the shiny refrigerators which were advertised in magazines. George understood that the attainment of the American Dream was beyond the grasp of his parents. But, there was one thing

> George trusted completely—his nation's military power and the good that it did. With all his heart he believed the United States, was on the side of justice and freedom and all our wars were noble. Despite personal hardships, you could always count on Americans, you could always count on Americans to be the good guys and always victorious. It was simply unimaginable that the United States might betray that faith.[36]

Very few non-Americans understand the centrality of the Vietnam War and the attendant inferno in the grandiloquent American experience. It should be tackled in such a manner that the tale and the halo surrounding the Vietnam War does not ascribe itself to only negativity, but the bounden positivity about the duty and the patriotic verve of the American experience with a global responsibility, too, needs to be a paramount concern. The Americans had to intervene due to the exigencies of the traditional cold war confrontation with the tardy communists. The Vietnam War ought not to be construed as a staid reckoning, but ought to be a kind of lullaby that appeals to the national interest argument and the patriotic streak among the Americans in the light of the media-hyped Vietnam carnage. The efficacy of the American intervention ought to be looked into with diligence in the light of the highlight of the Vietnam War.

Years after the war in Vietnam, conditions have changed drastically with the American perception of a Soviet takeover becoming a reality though in a post-cold war scenario, where-in the Soviets have lost the wherewithal to confront the Americans. The *Economist* reports, 'After the American withdrawal and communist triumph, the government of the newly reunited Vietnam leased the naval base to the Soviet Union. Russia gave up the facility in 2002. Today it is Russian tourists who flock to Cam Ranh International Airport, with its American-built airstrip, on their way to the beaches of nearby Nha Trang'.[37] How times have changed!!!!

The *Economist* further reports,

> These days Vietnam ostensibly follows a policy of 'Three Nos': no military alliances, no foreign bases and no joining with another country to fight a third. Nonetheless, adjacent to the Vietnamese naval base at Cam Ranh is a facility that receives foreign military vessels. In theory it is a purely commercial venture, open to the ships of any country willing to pay for the maintenance and refuelling, which, it provides. But, it also serves a strategic purpose: sending a defiant message to a resurgent

> and expansionist China by allowing Vietnam to strengthen military ties with an increasingly diverse group of countries.[38]

Vietnam in the year 2017 now follows an independent foreign policy trajectory. Akin to Japan, being wary of the vicissitudes of the Vietnam War, the national establishment makes a discernible attempt to stay clear of the entangling that is, alliances in a manner that Vietnam too follows the ideals of the old adversary, America's founding fathers.

Whatever might be the strivings of America's national interest argument, any self-respecting American denizen would have liked his nation to win the war. It's the patriotic zeal that needs to be delved inside as being a dissenter is an easy exercise down the trail, but being a firm believer in the efficacy of the national uprightness and the zeal of the American Dream, is a totally and grossly, different perspective of the entire facet of the narrative.

Stephen J Morris, wrote in the *New York Times*,

> The most popular explanation among historians and journalists is that the defeat was a result of American policy makers' cold-war-driven misunderstanding of North Vietnam's leaders as dangerous Communists. In truth, they argue, we were fighting a nationalist movement with great popular support. In this view, 'our side', South Vietnam, was a creation of foreigners and led by a corrupt urban elite with no popular roots. Hence it could never prevail, not even with a half-million American troops, making the war, 'unwinnable'.[39]

The fact that half a million troops could not prevent an American defeat speaks volumes about the planning and strategy part of the American intervention in Vietnam. The gross gaffe on the part of the Americans being that Americans misconstrued the war with a conflict in a Plain Jane manner against the Communist Internationale and not a nationalist uprising that had strong roots in the national lore and the related hinterland.

What needs to be comprehended is the notion that the true nature of the conflict and the ideological inclination of the Viet Cong was either underestimated by Washington or a complete pogrom of the Viet Cong eluded the comprehension of the Vietnam conflict. Morris writes,

> What is also clear from Soviet archival sources is that those who believed that North Vietnam had more than national unification on its mind were right: Its leaders were imbued with a sense of their ideological mission—not only to unify Vietnam under Communist Party rule,

> but also to support the victory of Communists in other nations. They saw themselves as the outpost of world revolution in Southeast Asia and desired to help Communists in Cambodia, Laos, Thailand and elsewhere.[40]

It is reported through other sources that the even the Soviets and their Naval contingents with their bosses were given a short shrift by the Vietnamese authorities in a bid to develop an individual, singularly independent and sovereign framework for the Vietnamese nation and its hoi polloi.

Morris concludes,

> In 1974-75, the United States snatched defeat from the jaws of victory. Hundreds of thousands of our Vietnamese allies were incarcerated, and more than a million driven into exile. The awesome image of the United States was diminished, and its enemies were thereby emboldened, drawing the United States into new conflicts by proxy in Afghanistan, Africa and Latin America. And the bitterness of so many American war veterans, who saw their sacrifices so casually demeaned and unnecessarily squandered, haunts American society and political life to this day.[41]

What can be conveniently surmised is that the United States entered into an epoch of an quintessential war-induced 'Vietnam Syndrome'. The much talked about Vietnam Syndrome has been an IR pet peeve since the seventies and has left an indelible impact upon the Cultural and Cinematic lore and depictions in the United States with the quintessential John Rambo rebelling against the American GI conception of nationhood when the American war veteran does not get an acceptable nod from the American establishment. Their grouses and grievances remain etched in the cultural and cinematic memory of the nation. Thus, the Oliver Stone movie, 'Born on the Fourth of July' makes a rendering of the American angst and the ferment that the American society underwent in the turbulent and vitriolic seventies.

Roger Bert reviews the character of the film and contends,

> Kovic came back from the war with a shattered body, but it took a couple of years for the damage to spread to his mind and spirit. By the time he hit bottom he was a demoralized, spiteful man who sought escape in booze and drugs and Mexican whorehouses. Then he began to look outside of himself for a larger pattern to his life, the pattern that inspired his best-selling autobiography, Born on the Fourth of July.[42]

The pantheon that the movie portrays presents a rather negative visage of the Vietnam War, and largely, the nation itself that should not be construed as the final word on the state of the nation during the heydays of Vietnam War. In a set piece in the movie, the male protagonist scolds his brother and implores upon him to be a patriotic citizen rather than gang up with the commies but when asked to deliver a speech on a nationalistic veteran's platform, he gets overawed by a hallucination of overhead choppers as the US soldiers disappear into the tropics spewing war cries in anticipation of a military engagement with the VC. Such was the impact of the all subsuming war!!!! But, it had to be fought against the Viet Cong.

The hallucination showcases that Ron Kovic, played by the popular Hollywood star, Tom Cruise, suddenly seems overawed by the sight and sound of a chopper in a Vietnamese battlefield, and words fail him, when his opportunity to deliver a rousing and patriotic speech for the townlings on a colourfully festooned stage comes. Apart from this set piece, the falling apart of the American Dream, with the manicured lawns and the wooden mail boxes along with the chatter of daintily clad kids in the housefronts with hot barbeques, enters the frame and remains with the audience for a long time to come.

The Moral Interventionist Take

Moral Interventionism and the Responsibility to Protect, are, the twin paradigms upon which the interventionism of America in Vietnam is premised. On a lighter side, when Uncle Ben breathes the last after being shot and mugged by a thief, then, he utters his last words, 'With Great Power Comes Great Responsibility'. These last words in the movie called 'Spiderman' has a life-transforming impact upon the male protagonist, Peter Parker, who is until now experimenting with his new-found powers and is yet to evolve into a full-fledged superhero, the Spiderman. Thus, the nuanced posturing that the anointed United States of America has, happens to be that of, a responsible nation state actor that posits a challenge to forces threatening peace, liberty, equity and an egalitarian ethos in the nation and the entire international system.

The war in Vietnam was a celebration of the ideals of the American Declaration of Independence and the anointed pelf of the superpower, that is, the United States of America. The Vietnam case study too reflects the R2P facet of US Foreign Policy with adumbrations that do not let the American interventions turn into 'Mission Creeps'.

It is always the case of moral interventionism pitted against the tenets of international law, where-in America's practical morality is questioned repeatedly. Immanuel Kant writes,

> Since at least the 18th century, the question of which disciplinary framework offers the most fruitful means for thinking about war and peace has been the subject of critical reflection. Immanuel Kant, for example, famously dismissed the possibility that lawyers such as Grotius, Pufendorf, and Vattel could offer any insights into the troubled question of how peace might be achieved on this earth. For Kant such lawyers were merely 'sorry comforters'.[43]

Thus, peacemaking in the context of United States is an avowed and qualificatory vocation and objective of the United States. Thus, in the American perspective and the larger perspective, the ordering principle of liberal internationalism is the order of the day, as, in the sixties after the Gulf of Tonkin Resolution, the United States of America attempted to outdo the exigencies of the Viet Cong in Northern Vietnam. The avowed zeal was the containment of the Warsaw group of nations, only that the gruesome nature of the struggle of the Vietnamese rebels turned the heat all the way to the American establishment in the larger international visage. The Cinematic depiction of the Pentagon Papers expose are assiduously and efficiently reflected in Steven Spielberg's biopic, *The Post*. It is here that the drawing room of Katherine Graham filled with the hard at work, *Washington Post* senior staff along with the arguments with the US Attorney General with Tom Hanks, come to the fore with the factual history of what the brouhaha over the Pentagon Paper expose was all about. As an aside, the unflinching rivalry between *The New York Times* which was much larger in circulation and the *Washington Post* in the frenzy being the first exposers, gets a great accord in the film's doughty narrative.

It can be assessed and analyzed that the morality argument militates against the functionalism of International Law. It should not be comprehended such that what all is not objectively inclined and international law cannot be included as part of the international narrative, and also, the morality idiom is only a myth that is much too utopian in nature and candour. Anne Orford writes in the article 'Moral Internationalism and Responsibility to Protect',

> The UN Charter was supposed to be the constitution of a new world, but, for reasons that have often been discussed, things have turned out

> differently. To dwell at length upon the precise meaning of the Charter is today a kind of utopian quibbling. And because the UN sometimes pretends that it already is what it has barely begun to be, its decrees do not command intellectual or moral respect—except among the positivist lawyers whose business it is to interpret them. The lawyers have constructed a paper world, which fails at crucial points to correspond to the world the rest of us still live in.[44]

Thus, the author too believes that positivist lawyers have too much of a clausewise reading involved in the narrative where-in the fall of the Vietnamese domino would have led to the next risk to be situated against its own homeland.

Another issue that the United States raised through its intervention in Vietnam was the rubric of humanitarian intervention. The US witnessed anarchic domestic behaviour by both the state and non-state actors that made it transform its presence in Vietnam from an advisory proposition to a full-fledged military intervention. It was all about a diplomatic moral conviction that the United States was acting in good faith and with a yeomanly objective for containing communist anarchy in the Indo-China. Walzer writes,

> Humanitarian intervention is justified when it is a response (with reasonable expectations of success) to acts 'that shock the moral conscience of mankind'. The old-fashioned language seems to me exactly right. It is not the conscience of political leaders that one refers to in such cases. They have other things to worry about and may well be required to repress their normal feelings of indignation and outrage. The reference is to the moral convictions of ordinary men and women, acquired in the course of everyday activities. And given that one can make a persuasive argument in terms of those convictions, I don't think that there is any moral reason to adopt that posture of passivity that might be called waiting for the UN (waiting for the universal state, waiting for the messiah...).[45]

An analysis of the legality of the US role in the Vietnam conflict ultimately polarizes into two separate aspects: (1) the constitutionality of the President's actions with regard to Vietnam, and (2) the validity of the intervention in the conflict under international law. While these two aspects of the problem are in some ways interdependent,[46] 'The international and constitutional consequences of the exercise of the foreign relations power are not identical'.[47] This difference in consequences is especially significant in view of the challenges that have been issued against the legality of the 'war'. The question of the legality of the American war in Vietnam has been raised ample of times counting in the debates around interventionism carried on by great powers such as the United States. The constitutional powers of the American President, too, cannot be questioned as the US Constitution makes the American President as the supreme commander of the defence forces along with the intercessions of the US Congress that together completes the war's clarion call in any conflict situation in the United States.

To date, the American judiciary has received cases questioning the validity and profundity of the American President's power and the correctness of the decision to go to war. These cases have not been conceded importance in the larger jurisprudence of the American nation apart from collaborating with the civil societal anti-war movement in America. William N Nobel writes, 'To date, the courts have uniformly refused to hear these cases, stating that the petitioners lack proper standing to raise the issue of the legality of the "war", and further that the issues involved are inherently non-justiciable'.[48] Thus, the American courts in a way have declared the private personages as the persona non grata in a manner to be capable enough to wage a protest against the American decision to wage a war against the State of Vietnam. The courts also find these issues non-justiciable and away from the parlour of the courts.

A stealthy figment of law can be cited with the appellation that four American Presidents have ascribed military assistance to South Vietnam since the last 15 years. A few sources along with President Johnson's speech can be cited over here in the contemporary context. The sources contend, 'With regard to Vietnam itself, beginning in 1954 some precedent has been established by the fact that four Presidents have prescribed military assistance to South Vietnam for the past fifteen years. Thus, it appears that if the Constitution can be interpreted by practice, the President's actions with regard to Vietnam would be justified'.[49] This appears to be a valid and necessary rule if any degree of stability is to be maintained in governmental functions. The Court retreated from this position in *Youngstown Skeet & Tube Co. v. Sawyer*, however, when it held that President Truman's seizure of a private enterprise in order to settle a labour dispute could not be justified by the fact that prior Presidents had acted in a similar manner without Congressional authority.[50]

Article 4 of the Constitution imparts Treaties, the status of the law of the land.[51] It should follow, *a fortiori*, that the Executive may not constitutionally violate any treaty provisions. The pragmatic value of this limitation, however, is doubtful. The President's broad, plenary power to determine the foreign policy of this country has long been recognized.[52] When the President acts in the foreign relations field, courts have consistently refused to review his actions. Thus, since the case of *Ware v. Hylon*, decided by the Supreme Court in 1796, the courts of this country have uniformly held that it is not for the judiciary to determine whether the President has broken a treaty, or even whether a treaty has been terminated or is still in existence. Thus, the Courts have generally castigated the protests against the establishment's decision to go to war. All in all, the Presidential prerogative to decide about going to war had been witnessed a multiple of times, thus, entailing a kind of go ahead for the American President. It has been accepted through the jurisprudence of America, too, that the United States of America and its President have all the sovereign right to amalgamate with the world trend to decide about one's own nation's foreign policy. Snatching away that prerogative would be Un-American and non-epochal.

It's a well planned out and still panning out in the contemporary context, blame game, as far as the allegation that the United States should not have intervened in Vietnam, is concerned. Some of the global observers of IR and conflict/peace studies have gone on to augue about this debate 'whether great powers such as United States keep on intervening in the corpus of conflict centres such as Vietnam'. Still, it can be safely asserted that no one in the United States enjoys the clean chit as far as interventions are concerned, but, it is the sovereign right of a nation state and its political leadership that apart from allowing a free run in the domestic public sphere, the establishment of that power sustains the right to manage its independent foreign policy. The nation is enjoined with a rigid right that it can exercise its sovereign discretion to declare war or make peace with an adversary nation. Thus, what the United States did in Vietnam also reflects that strategic autonomy of the grandiloquent United States of America.

Apart from the narrative of the debate, the American penchant for stressing upon and living their "American Dream" runs supreme and runs ramshod over the dictum of allegations and staid vituperations. The Vietnam War should not be extolled as a mere test case of American military might, technological and communication finesse. It was much more than that. The Vietnam War was about the value laden-conception of being a do-gooder nation state and the details should run more than as a mere debate upon the wrongfulness or the incorrectness of the debate. The Americans were faced with a cold-war conditionality. They had to carve out a safe residence for the Diem executive functionality in the Global realm.

Thus, in many ways, the American establishment had to employ diplomatic stealth in the beginning and then adhere on to military interventionism in order to live up to its avowed credentials of moral internationalism. Any nation must be inclined over time to strike out on its own and with coalitions of willing in order to serve its national interest. The Global liberal charge would have been that the United States was a mute spectator to the antics of Ho Chi Minh, if the South Vietnamese regime would not have been bolstered by Washington. Vietnam should not be remembered for its carnage and the dubious allegation of the carnage falling flat on the face of Washington, but if the left randomization remains limited to the Interventionism debate, then that would be a levelling and overawing facet of the historic Vietnam War.

NOTES

1. Landsberg, Brian K., 'The United States in Vietnam: A Case Study in the Law of Intervention', *California Law Review*, 50(3), August 1962.
2. Ibid.
3. Press Conference of 17 November 1961, in 45 Dep't State Bull. 920 (1961).
4. Address by Secretary of State Rusk, Davidson College, 22 February 1962, in 46 Dep't State Bun. 450 (1962).
5. 31 Dep't State Bull. 162 (1954).
6. The State Department says, 'the present balance of forces between independent and Communist states in Asia would be tipped perilously if Viet-Nam, Cambodia, and Laos fell under Communist domination. What then would be the prospects for Thailand and Burma, for Pakistan and India, for Malaya and Indonesia?'
7. *New York Times*, 28 April 1962, p. 1, column 8.
8. The statements cannot be explained away as mere off-the-cuff remarks. The State Department is aware of the scrutiny given its statements and is accordingly careful and reflective in making them. Then-Acting Secretary of State Ball has made this quite clear: 'No responsible officer of the Department of State can make a public statement about world affairs without being aware that he is speaking to more than one audience. Whatever he says to Americans regarding the thrust and purpose of any aspect of foreign policy will be meticulously studied in the chanceries of the world'. Address by Acting Secretary of State Ball to the Northwestern Law Alumni Ass'n, 9 May 1962, in 46 Dep't State Bull. 872, 873 (1961).
9. In a story dated 27 February 1962, the *New York Times* said, 'The Soviet Union warned today that United States military action against Communist guerrillas in South Vietnam involved a possibility of "alarming consequences" for world peace' (p. 1, col. 8). The Soviet Foreign Ministry has said the American action 'creates a serious threat to the peace in that region'. *The New York Times*, 18 March 1962, p. 30, col. 1.
10. *The New York Times*, 28 April 1962, p. 1, col. 8.

11. President Kennedy's Press Conference of 11 October 1961, in 19 CONe. *QUAR.* 1742 (1961).
12. Tanham Communist Revolutionary Warfare 111 (1961).
13. Clubb, *Trap in Vietnam,* The Progressive, April 1962, p. 16. See also 'A Threat to the Peace', pt. I, pp. 7–11.
14. 'War Crimes Law and the Vietnam War Archived', 2008-05-09 at the Wayback Machine., Benjamin B. Ferencz, *The American University Law Review,* 17(3), 1968.
15. The Abandonment of International Law After 9/11, Richard Falk, 21 Septemeber 2005.
16. US Supreme Court, *Sarnoff v. Schultz,* No. 71-1652 (1972), Argued N/A Decided, 16 October 1972.
17. McLaughlin, Katie, 'The Vietnam War: The Five things, You Might Not Know'. http://edition.cnn.com/2014/06/20/us/vietnam-war-five-things/. Accessed 28 May 2017.
18. Ibid.
19. Ibid.
20. Quora, 'Why Did America Really Get Involved in the Vietnam War'. https://www.quora.com/Why-did-America-really-get-involved-with-the-Vietnam-War. Accessed 28 May 2017.
21. US Government, National Archives, Pentagon Papers, 1972.
22. Pentagon Papers, US Involvement in the War, Internal Documents, the Kennedy Administration: January 1961–December 1963, Chronological Lists of Documents.
23. Pentagon Papers, Geneva Accords, US Military Planning and Diplomatic Maneuver, January–July, 1954.
24. Ibid.
25. Ibid.
26. Babones, Salvator, 'American Hegemony Is Here to Stay', *National Interest,* 11 June 2015.
27. Ibid.
28. Ibid.
29. W.W. 'The World Order: The Stakes of American Hegemony', 12 February 2012.
30. Riggio, Ronald, 'The Top 10 Leadership Competencies', *Psychology Today,* 14 April 2014.
31. Ibid.
32. Aristotle (trans. by Martin Ostwald), *Nicomachean Ethics,* CT, USA: Martino Fine Books, 2016.
33. Duong, David, 'Forty Years after the Vietnam War'. http://www.huffingtonpost.com/david-duong/40-years-after-the-vietna_b_7162546.html. Accessed 28 May 2017.
34. Ibid.
35. Donnelly, Thomas, 'The Ghosts of Saigon and Baghdad'. https://www.aei.org/publication/the-ghosts-of-saigon-and-baghdad/. Accessed 28 May 2017.
36. Appy, Christian G., *American Reckoning: The Vietnam War and Our National Identity,* New York: Penguin, 2015, p. 1.
37. 'Vietnam Uses an Old Naval Base to Make New Friends', *The Economist,* 20 April 2017.
38. Ibid.
39. Morris, Stephen J., 'The War We Could Have Won', *The New York Times,* 1 May 2005.
40. Ibid.
41. Ibid.
42. Ebert, Roger, 'Born on the Fourth of July'. http://www.rogerebert.com/reviews/born-on-the-fourth-of-july-1989. Accessed 1 May 2017.
43. Kant, 'Perpetual Peace: A Philosophical Sketch', in *Kant: Political Writings,* H.S. Reiss (ed.), Cambridge: Cambridge University Press, 1970.

44. Orford, Anne, 'Moral Responsibility and the Right to Protect', *European Journal of International Law*, 24 (1), 2013, pp. 83–108.
45. Walzer, M., *Just and Unjust Wars: A Moral Argument with Historical Illustrations* (4th ed.), 2006, xxiii.
46. See, generally, Wright, *Legal Aspects of the Viet-Nam Situation*, 60 Am. J. INT'L L. 750 (1966); Falk, International Law and the United States Role in the Viet Nam War, 75 YALE L.J. 1122 (1966).
47. Moore, *International Law and the United States Role in Viet Nam: A Reply*, 76 YALE L.J. 1051, 1092 (1967); see *Chae Chan Ping v. United States*, 130 U.S. 581 (1889) *Whitney v. Robertson*, 124 U.S. 190 (1888).
48. Ibid.
49. Nobel, Willaim N., 'The Legality of United State's Involvement in Vietnam: A Pragmatic Approach', *University of Miami Law Review*, 23(4/7), 1969.
50. See, generally, Staff of Senate Committee on Foreign Relations, *Background Information Relating to Southeast Asia and Vietnam*, 90th Cong., 2nd Sess. (4th rev. ed. Comm. Print 1968); Address by President Johnson on America's Efforts Toward World Order, A.B.A., 12 August 1964, in 51 Dep't State Bull. 298, 299 (1964).
51. *United States v. Midwest Oil Co.*, 236 U.S. 459 (1915). The Court based its opinion on the premise that citizens naturally adjust themselves to any long-continued action of the Executive Department, on the presumption that unauthorized acts would not have been allowed to be so often repeated as to crystallize into a regular practice.
52. *Missouri v. Holland*, 252 U.S. 416 (192).
53. *United States v. Belmont*, 301 U.S. 324, 330 (1937).

8

Iraq Reconsidered With or Without the United States

JUSTICE Cascade is a notion advanced by Sikkink, which refers to the new-found recalcitrance of the third-world nations. Earlier on, the developing nations would sit quietly while the various hyper-nations ran riot in the global landscape. Now, the myriad developing states are part of the 'Justice Cascade', which, aims to challenge the superpuissance of the superpowers of the order of the United States of America. The US itself ought to preach and practice alike about the 'Justice Cascade' while intervening abroad in the name of its higher value laden foreign policy.

In the line of American interventions, comes the leapfrogging conflict of Iraq. Iraq as a nation has been witness to political changes and transformations with the Regimes before Saddam Hussein, Persian Gulf Wars I and II and the rise of the ISIS, being part of the process of American intervention in the badlands of Mesopotamia. But, American interventions are no longer being considered as the last rites of Count Dracula. Iraq under Saddam Hussein emerged as the receptacle of Islamic power with the rivals being the Sharia State of Iran. Iraq was found housing the WMDs and Saddam Hussein was found to have working links and functional affinity with Al Qaeda, which founded the American premise of waging the 'War-on-Terror', by the American establishment under the suzerainty of President Bush, Jr, who was much lampooned by the International Media on the perceived want of an IQ and intellect in the context of Persian Gulf War II in March 2003.

What can be pondered over is that the United States was able to get the global consensus through the United Nations through a slew of UNSC Resolutions that made the United Nations legally pass the American intervention in 1991 in the Iraq–Kuwait crisis. The same WMD excuse in the aftermath of the IAEA in-charge giving a clean chit to Iraq was not used to give a complete permission to US and its allies in the war to undo Saddam Hussein in 2003. There is an often-cited want of the second UNSC resolution that led the United States and its 'Coalition of the Willing' to launch a tirade against the Iraq's claim to leadership in West Asia. Thus, the second military intervention of Iraq in March 2003 as an aftermath of the WMD ruse was made functional without the sanction of the United Nations. This want of the UN sanction largely undermines the brave new front of nations attempting to cobble together a front against Global Jihad and utter terror that now threatens the European terrain as the new battleground in terror busting.

Some of the IR and US policy observers feared that the American Operations 'Desert Storm' and 'Enduring Freedom' would bring back the memories of the debacle in Vietnam, but the American victory in 1991, in the Persian Gulf War, lifted the Americans out of the dreaded and stultifying, Vietnam syndrome that the Americans found themselves embroiled in, after the carnage of Vietnam War. Thus, the Americans were looking ahead for 'a redemptive occasion' to emerge out of the taint and the misery of Vietnam carnage. They were able to achieve with the defeat of Iraq in an overseas war with alien but definitively, national interest–oriented objectives. Thus, the twin Iraq wars were good reference points for anyone who is studying the American involvement in Iraq that was despairingly disparaged as 'American invasions' in the nation state of Iraq with the vitriolic and damaging allegation of American floundering in Iraq leading to the rise of the Islamic State. It is in the larger public opinion mould too that the entire intervention in Iraq can be analysed and commented upon.

The Public Opinion Interlude

'Medium is the Message' is a popular saying advanced by Marshall McLuhan, one of the eminent media studies theorists.[1] Shanto Iyengar, in his seminal study *Is Anyone Responsible?* has further advanced the notion that media personalities involved are part of the reporting of news and events. This raises the question whether media has extended its coverage since the Persian Gulf

War I. It leads us on to describe and analyse the changes in war reporting during the intervening years. This segment would further seek to analyse the following argument: Objectivity and journalistic standards are compromised during wartime, or are they the first casualty during wartime. Through a detailed analysis of the US media coverage of Persian Gulf War II, the hypothesis that the media plays a vital and significant role in the national discourse during wartime can be examined. Finally, we can persist to examine the government–media relations by contrasting the practices prevalent in Gulf war I and the changes that occurred during Gulf War II.

The media has vastly extended its coverage of conflicts since Persian Gulf War I. Earlier on during Persian Gulf War I, only a 'pool of reporters' used to be employed near the battlefield. The new methodology of appointing an 'embedded group' of reporters has enhanced the expanse of the media coverage pertaining to the Persian Gulf War fought in the year 2003.[2] The movement and the sphere of operation of the media personnel has increased manifold that is aided by new global positioning satellite technologies and other advanced technologies.[3] The nature of stories being filed and the resultant debate that takes place, is a direct consequence of the increased coverage and the immediacy of the media coverage in the country. War becomes a satellite festival for the various media personnel with the all prominent news and events on the battlefield being covered with precision and in great detail.

During Persian Gulf War I, the war was widely covered but the media personnel had to rely upon the military releases and the press attaché's statements.[4] The war correspondents were not allowed to venture out with the troops and the warplanes to cover military missions.[5] This policy resulted in a scarcity of 'live feeds' for the spectators. During Persian Gulf War II, the embedded reporters were selectively allowed to venture with the military personnel during the military operations that resulted in a more in-depth and lively coverage of the war. Thus, apart from the Vietnam War, an interlude of recorded telecasts of My Lai with the monks' self-immolation in city squares and, the American GIs setting fire to huts brought an unavoidably large deluge of negative byte for the American establishment that still remains part of the scorched narrative on Vietnam and the attendant conflict.

Media reportage during peaceful times is an ordinary affair involving less of operational dangers of the battlefield. There is a complex social-systemic interlocking of militarism with other historical, political, institutional, economic, cultural and psychological forces. These factors tend to reinforce the hegemony of militarism and aggressive, pre-emptive foreign policy in the current period.[6] The Washington-based *Project for the New American Century* (PNAC)[7] is also an effort on the part of the American authorities for driving home the point of a pre-emptive war against the rogue states. It helped the conservative ideologues into structuring a rationale for war in March 2003. PNAC, a non-profit educational organization, was dedicated to a few fundamental propositions: that American leadership is good both for America and for the world and that such leadership required military strength, diplomatic energy and commitment to moral principles. It also included the argument that few American political leaders are making the case for global leadership that must change. Further more, it was committed to promoting American world leadership and notably to the control of international cyberspace. The philosophical underpinnings of these neo-conservatives are acknowledged to be in the writings of political theorists such as Machiavelli, Hobbes and Edmund Burke.[8] The question was, how much of these arguments were reflected in the media portrayal of Gulf War II. Thus, the neo-conservative thought, which was the mainstay of the American interventions in Iraq, was brought forth and amply targeted by the liberal media as the arch dark lights of the conflict. Neo-conservatism paraded about by the likes of personages such as Donald Rumsfeld and others were lampooned and castigated by the liberal press both inside and outside the confines of the United States of America. But, that is how a hyper and super power behaves in global service.

The Concept of Embedded Reporting

Some of the reporters in Iraq during wartime were embedded and others were independent. The term given to individual correspondents was *unilaterals.* The central theme of most of the stories with these 'embeds' was that how bad the conditions were and why the reporters were exhausted and had to go home after their gruelling 5 weeks of covering the war.[9] Observers have marvelled at the courage and fortitude of the military personnel who endured these conditions for months on end. Some of the stories reflect admiration for the troops and an increased appreciation of the US military and the difficult conditions under which they work and fight. Some stories reflect a lack of preparedness and understanding by the reporters of what they were going to undertake in Iraq.

In comparison with the Gulf War of 1991, the war in 2003, was more wide-open for reporters. This was partly done to counteract propaganda emanating from the Iraqi government. It was also an attempt to control and influence the news by keeping journalists under close watch. The Pentagon developed a 'slick new public relations concept known as embedding'. Embedded reporting was a new phenomenon that was developed to facilitate the media coverage of the war as the correspondents accompanied the fighting units in the battlefield.

A few observers like Katovsky and Carlson,[10] interviewed 60 leading journalists who lived, ate and travelled with the American troops. The authors began with a brief history of the relationship between the military and the media and a discussion of the practice of embedding reporters detailing the pros and cons. The interviews included *CBS News*' Jim Axelrod who mourned the loss of his colleague David Bloom[11] and Peter Baker belonging to the *Washington Post.* Axelrod recalled the strain of covering a battle while worrying about his wife Susan Glasser who was also reporting from Iraq. Recollections ranged from the raw fear provoked by close calls in the battlefield to the boredom of daily briefings at the CENTCOM media centre in Doha, Qatar.[12]

During the build-up to the war in Iraq, Secretary of Defense, Donald Rumsfeld faced an important decision regarding the military's Public Affairs policy. He needed to decide the way in which the war would be covered by radio, television and print media. The Defence Secretary advanced three courses of action:

- He could continue the practice of limiting the media's access to the battlefield and conduct press briefings at the Pentagon and during Operation Enduring Freedom.
- Secretary Rumsfeld could employ a second option that envisioned a return to the management of the media through the creation and use of media pools as had been done during Operation Desert Shield/ Desert Storm.
- A third course of action suggested, was, that the Department of Defence (DoD) and the military leverage the media used were an extremely radical public affairs plan now referred to as 'the embedded media program'. In the year 2004, another set of interrogation documents were released by the Department of Defense in the form of a memo.[13]

In consultation with the Assistant Secretary of Defense for Public Affairs, Victoria Clarke,[14] Secretary Rumsfeld chose to implement the embedded media program because he understood that the media coverage of the impending war would 'shape public perception of the national security environment'. The technology used by the media to report instantaneously from distant locations with the rise of non-American news agencies (specifically the Arab news agency, *Al Jazeera*) overpowered military public relations efforts.The American and international media needed to have freedom of access and reporting free of the restrictive nature of press pools and without necessary censorship. Secretary Rumsfeld announced his decision in his Public Affairs Guidance message dated 10 February 2003, 'We need to tell the factual story, good or bad, before others seed the media with disinformation...'.

The American Rationale in the War with Iraq

The role of the media in explaining the causes for American intervention in Iraq is worth explaining. Many media houses attempted to be in the good books of the administration in its objectives and the government prompted some of the newspaper and television channels to pepper their pro-government coverage with articles of anti-war analysis. The critiques also pointed out that such media often questioned the governmental decisions regarding minor issues and did not raise questions about major issues such as 'the rationale advanced by the government to undertake the war' and 'the liberal and democratic ideal involved in intervening in a far-off land'.

This argument continued to point out that the Bush administration's justification for an invasion based on the claim that Iraq posed an imminent military threat, was open to many questions. It prompted discussions in the media that the failure of UN inspectors to find evidence of Iraqi weapons of mass destruction was a major setback for the administration and had fuelled public scepticism towards the administration's war.[15] Many ideological critics of Bush administration, also wrote that events in Korea further undermined the White House propaganda campaign. The Bush administration spokesmen have been unable to explain the disparity between the American policy towards North Korea and the war drive against Iraq.[16]

The US administration insisted that North Korea, which had openly declared that it was developing a nuclear weapons capacity, was to be dealt through diplomatic channels. But Iraq, where there was no evidence of nuclear weapons, had to be attacked and militarily occupied. Such differences in approach in Iraq however were not questioned and critically examined by the media. This war involving precious American lives in a far-off land littered with dangers, was not informed by the media. According to Pew Research Center polls, citizens of the country were ill-informed and unaware of the stakes involved in the West Asia, due to such bad reporting. The Israel–Palestine conflict had always been their focus of attention and debate in the West Asia,[17] and the media reporting was termed inadequate on the Iraq War. In particular, as the reasons advanced by Bush administration were found to be replete with falsehoods, the media role once again became the focus of sustained scrutiny. As the foreign policy of Bush administration and the strategies it undertook to achieve its goals became hotly contested in the US, media's coverage of foreign policy itself began to be probed. Thus, as part of the narrative on the American intervention in the battle over Iraq with a regime change in the offing, the media coverage of the Iraq wars remains an interesting and vital source for gleaning the sources of American conduct in the badlands of Mesopotamia.

The Dynamics of the UN Sanctions in Iraq

Whenever the United States intervenes in a conflict in a far-off land, the attendant dynamics of domestic politics, too, plays a role in the decision to go to war and the further sustainability of that decision related to an intervention. Paul R Pillar writes,

> Another common misconception is that politicization consists of intelligence officers being pushed in one incorrect direction rather than the opposite correct direction. The Iraqi WMD issue was far more complex than a Commission like the Senate Intelligence Committee or the Silberman Robb Commission. The familiar WMD label embraced a variety of programs or suspected clandestine programmes, including nuclear chemical and biological weapons as well as delivery systems. Each programme presented multiple sub issues such as the Regime's intent to pursue the program, the current state of development work, the status of production of weapons, the number or amount of any weapons already in existence and the timetable for producing weapons not made as yet.[18]

Thus, the American case for the war in Iraq was one of the spawning of the WMDs by the Saddam Regime in a quest for regional dominance and tradeoffs with the other West Asian actors in a state of nuclear blackmail. A great deal of debate and deliberations went on too in the US Congress related to this then-novae theme of the spawning of WMDs by the Saddam Hussein Regime.

Pillar further writes,

> The Political master's intense desire to make the case for war, their need to make the case to muster sufficient support for the war they already had decided to launch – pervaded every interaction between policy makers and intelligence officers that had anything to do with the Iraq war. The welcome that awaited any material and any judgments that supported the public case for war and the disfavor that met anything inconsistent with the case were all too obvious. The pro war wind that Bush administration had generated blew through all the corridors of Government, including the ones in which intelligence officers worked. The wind was strong, unrelenting and inescapable.[19] Still, the threat to the homeland could not be underplayed and given a short shrift.

The entire America seemed to be under the corpus of the 'Rally Around the Flag Phenomenon', where-in the idiom of the entire nation congregating around the national cause of war became the paramount concern. This phenomenon of 'Rally Around the Flag' has been a characteristic factor in the American response to crisis and threat to the homeland in the analysis undertaken by the Pew Research Centre and a few other public poll set-ups.

Some observers of the war in Iraq were suing the nomenclature that the Bush administration was spinning a yarn but the White House adhered to its conditioned argument that there was a palpable threat to the American homeland. The 'spinning the yarn' theme can be further elucidated upon. It goes without saying that all the public officials were involved in demonizing Iraq, but that kind of manicheastic rendition was being attempted by the Baghdad Regime, too. The Americans were contending that they were pre-empting the threat to the homeland by a dictator gone mad. The Cheney speech and other utterances by the various personages can be delved inside with some insinuation.

One senior military officer later commented about the speeches, 'When the Vice President stood up and said, that we are sure, well who are we to argue?'[20] The following month, as intelligence community analysts were preparing their estimates on the subject, Donald Rumsfeld publicly declared to a Senate Committee that Saddam's Regime had an active programme to acquire and develop nuclear weapons and had amassed large, clandestine stockpiles of chemical weapons. He pronounced in similarly certain, unqualified tones at the very moment, that, intelligence community analysts were deliberating about their differences and preparing their estimate on the subject.[21]

Another term that was utilized for the Intelligence controversy about the infallibility of the American information on WMDs was that of 'sexed up' intelligence that reflected the lie that allegedly lay embedded in the American efforts vis-à-vis Saddam Hussein. Even Judith Miller, the *New York Times* journalist, visited a couple of chemicals facilities in Baghdad and found utilizable centrifuges in the factories.[22] Thus, there was evidence hinting towards something more sinister that pervaded the American rationale to go to war.

What needs to be comprehended, is that there is a harsh prognosis for the American intent and the related foreign policy fundamentals that foreign adversaries will withhold secrets that are most impenetrable to the most skilled efforts to obtain them.Much of what would be most useful to know involves the complex interplay of various factors, the outcome of which is unpredictable. One can delimit the scope of uncertainty by contending that the American decision to negate the merry-go-round of terror spectacles and modules was late alright. Since the advent of the September 11 terror catastrophe, it was the requirement of the American homeland and the security of the nation that biblical and unprecedented steps were embarked on by the American establishment.

The United States had to learn to stop wars before they start and that was exactly the idea behind the theme of Preventive Diplomacy and Pre-emption. Lord David Owen writes in a book,

> 'The Greek Physician Herophilus observed some two thousand years ago that illness renders science null, art inglorious, strength effortless, wealth useless and eloquence powerless. Conflict does the same thing to the body politic. Conflict is cancerous in the way it erodes democracy and trust and civilized values. Preventing is very different from curing illness, and preventive health has acquired over the centuries different skills from resolving conflict and even they cannot always be separated out. Yet, diplomats, akin to physicians, have not developed a preventive ethos and a disciplined method of working.[23]

Peacenik strivings happen to be the order of the day and what the Doctor has called for. Article 33 of the UN Charter obligates member states to seek peaceful settlements of any dispute that may endanger international peace and security.[24]

The Security Council is empowered by Article 34 to investigate not only such disputes but 'any situation that may lead to international friction or give rise to a dispute'. Any state can bring any dispute according to Article 35 to the attention of the Security Council and the General Assembly.[25] Thus, pre-empting a conflict and serving a warning before a situation gets out of hand is what the United States of America, was, attempting and assiduously striving to do that falls in tandem with the larger auspices of the mandate of the United Nation's values, principles, norms and the Charter that has clinically declared 'War to be a menace and a scourge of mankind'. Another propaganda that has been festooned atop the narrative of Iraq war happens to be that there was a great deal of mounting casualties as the war unfurled itself in the Mesopotamian wastes. This factoid does not hold much credence. Few people pointed out what Saddam Hussein might be up to. Tim Weiner published an article in *The Times* in 1999 that talked up the weapons threat as a counterpoint to the patient, long-term containment of Iraq that was the Clinton administration's policy towards Iraq, 'He may be as close to building a nuclear weapon—perhaps closer—than he was in 1991'.[26] Thus, the containment of Iraq apart from being a moralist intervention, had to be initiated as the regional balance of power situation too warranted that way with Saddam Hussein suddenly beginning to straddle the region with diktats and other arm-twisting policy pieces.

Another issue that equally goads and rankles the American establishment is that of the second resolution during Persian Gulf War II, where-in, the Americans and the rest of the 'Coalition of the Willing' could not arrange for the warring sanction of the UN Security Council. The, then Secretary General of the United Nations, Kofi Annan, contended that the war on Iraq was illegal and broached the mandate of the UN Charter. The newspaper *Guardian* premised in London, too, expressed its reading of the situation concerning reconstruction, rehabilitation and the stabilization of Iraq after the Dictatorial Regime had collapsed and the negotiations were on to usher in democracy in the state of Iraq.

The newspaper wrote,

> Mr Annan also questioned whether it will be feasible on security grounds

> to go ahead with the first planned election in Iraq scheduled for January. 'You cannot have credible elections if the security conditions continue as they are now'. His remarks come amid a marked deterioration of the situation on the ground, an upsurge of violence that has claimed 200 lives in four days and raised questions over the ability of the interim Iraqi government and the US-led coalition to maintain control over the country.[27]

Globally, too, some of the nations and the statesmen have expressed the idiom that Iraq was in breach of the UN resolutions pertaining to security and threat of war, especially the UNSC Resolution 1441 passed in 2002. The *Guardian* wrote,

> Both Mr Blair and the foreign secretary, Jack Straw, claim that Saddam Hussein was in breach of security council resolution 1441 passed late in 2002, and of previous resolutions calling on him to give up weapons of mass destruction. France and other countries claimed these were insufficient. No immediate comment was available from the White House late last night, but American officials have defended the war as an act of self-defence, allowed under the UN charter, in view of Saddam Hussein's supposed plans to build weapons of mass destruction.[28]

Thus, the American standpoint has always revolved around the notion of national interest and self-defence that militates against the soft policy on terrorism and insurgency that some of the nations harbour as key pedestals of their policy framework.

The Iraq War United Nations Security Council Resolution can be cited over here that bans war, threats to peace, quite clearly and in a well-delineated manner. Certain relevant and pro-democracy segments of the UNSC Resolution 1441 can be cited over here that posit the Iraqi State to be in the wrong with a breach of the ideals of the international order being the order of the day. The state and the Government of Iraq was looked down upon as it was found to be in violation of the select sections of the UNSC Resolution no. 687 that was passed in 1991 which pinpointedly blamed the Saddam Government of violating the complete disclosure clause of the UNSC Resolution 687. The relevant sections of the text of the Resolution are as follows:

> Recognizing the threat Iraq's non-compliance with Council resolutions and proliferation of weapons of mass destruction and long-range missiles poses to international peace and security, Recalling that its resolution

> 678 (1990) authorized Member States to use all necessary means to uphold and implement its resolution 660 (1990) of 2 August 1990 and all relevant resolutions subsequent to resolution 660 (1990) and to restore international peace and security in the area,[29] Further recalling that its resolution 687 (1991) imposed obligations on Iraq as a necessary step for achievement of its stated objective of restoring international peace and security in the area, Deploring the fact that Iraq has not provided an accurate, full, final, and complete disclosure, as required by resolution 687 (1991), of all aspects of its programmes[30] to develop weapons of mass destruction and ballistic missiles with a range greater than one hundred and fifty kilometres, and of all holdings of such weapons, their components and production facilities and locations, as well as all other nuclear programmes, including any which it claims are for purposes not related to nuclear-weapons-usable material.[31]

Another ticklish piece of legalese can be looked upon here. The portal Global Policy Forum informs us,

> Because the UN Security Council refused to endorse the US-UK invasion and occupation of Iraq in March 2003, Washington and London hoped to ignore the UN and operate with a free hand in the country. But, a fierce Iraqi resistance, persistent economic and political problems, and continuing international criticism forced the US-UK to seek international partners for their enterprise, including assistance from the UN. A debate ensued between those who thought that the UN could be the wedge for internationalization and US-UK withdrawal and those who thought that a UN presence would only discredit the world body.[32]

The portal further informs, 'Following the adoption of Security Council Resolution 1483 two months after the war, then-UN Secretary General Kofi Annan appointed a Special Representative for Iraq and the UN assumed some small responsibilities there. Many critics warned, though, that the UN should not be identified with the illegal war and occupation'.[33] The characterization of the American nature of action with the other coalition nations as being in the wrong and committing a gross illegality, is a fashionable academic cannon that needs to rejected and vehemently countered. The UNSC clearly also resolved to provide evidence that Saddam's regimewas not in consonance with the UNSC-declared international law and was culpable as a recalcitrant and a rogue nation. The term 'Rogue Nation' falls in tandem along with the rest of the International Law nomenclature, where-in it was not President George

Bush, Jr, who was the progenitor of this term, but, the other historically non-compliant nations, too, have been termed with the same nomenclature. It's not an quintessential American construct as some of the anarchist lawmakers would not think twice before painting the United States too with the same black and tainted brush of propaganda and ghastly left-wing prejudice.

The British Broadcasting Corporation (BBC) too informed the international audience that though there is no direct presence of WMDs in the Iraqi arsenal, but, still the investigators continue to hold that some of the loopholes need to be delved inside vis-à-vis the connection between WMDs and the Iraqi regime. The excerpt from BBC informs, 'On 7 March 2003 Hans Blix told the UN that Iraq had taken significant steps to comply with its disarmament obligations, but, said that there were still unanswered questions. He subsequently said that if asked he should have requested more time to complete his task'.[34] The message that has been erroneously communicated by the Global Media and partisan left wingers in the firmament with insane retentiveness happens to be that the IAEA inspectors provided a clean chit to the Saddam Regime, pointing that there was no presence of WMDs in the territory, and with the establishment of Iraq. Thus, the illegality of Iraq was never brought to the fore though it acted as an invader par excellence in Persian Gulf War I of 1991 when it too acted pre-emptively invading the territory of the nation state of Kuwait. Another blame game that the global left media keeps on harping about, as if intuitively, is that of the sanctions slapped by the West on the Iraqi regime. The Plain Jane argument has been that the Americans were attempting a regime change in Baghdad by cutting off the sinews of the Saddam Regime by creating a false paucity of day-to-day necessities and civic supplies in order to contraband the Iraqi government or to dismember the nation through inciting rebellion and dissatisfaction amongst the population.

The BBC report further contends that some measures relating to the taking of military action against Baghdad were essential if for the security and stolidity of the region, the complete Disarmament of Iraq was the need of the hour. The BBC report informs,

> He also warned that any military action 'must have as its objective the enforcement of the terms of the cease-fire' and 'must be a proportionate response to that objective, ie securing compliance with Iraq's disarmament obligations'. He added that 'regime change cannot be the objective of military action' although removing Saddam Hussein would be legal 'if it can be demonstrated that such action is a necessary and proportionate measure to secure the disarmament of Iraq'.[35]

Thus, the theme of attaining the disarmament of rogue nations, can be earmarked as one of the rationales for attacking Iraq with 'necessary and proportionate measures'. But, instead some sections of left-liberal media portrayed the American nation and its President in a manicheastic mould and harped upon the idea of the personage of Saddam Hussein being the victimized and avidly vilified personage, who, was earlier the national god head.

If President George Bush was tauntingly painted as being so uninformed that he could not locate India on a World Map, Saddam Hussein can be booked on more potent facts. It was one of the Government Hospitals in Kuwait City that some incubators in the maternity ward were torn asunder by the Iraqi soldiers in one of the most dastardly and inhuman acts of grime-crime. The incubators bearing newborns were damaged and that was the testimony of a lady from the nation of Kuwait. Such grime-filled visages were the order of the day and reporting and commenting upon them amounted to incarcerating the personage of Saddam Hussein in the larger media and the global polity.

The war was also painted as the thesis of the Clash of Civilizations wherein, the Islamic and the American nations were pitted against each other ala the historic narrative of Crusades. Still, one has to accept grudgingly the order of the day that in the aftermath of the UNSC Resolution 1441, a completing UNSC resolution was required to silence most of the international lawyers. BBC further reports, 'Resolution 1441 would have provided that a further decision of the Security Council to sanction force was required if that had been intended. All it requires is reporting to and discussion by the Security Council of Iraq's failures, but not an express further decision to authorise force'.[36] Thus, an additional protocoled vision and an addendum were required to grant a complete currency to the American and the Coalition's 'War on terror' in the nation state of Iraq. Succor can be found in a particular section of the UNSC Resolution 1441 that the combined impact of the UNSC legalese during the days of Persian Gulf War I could be the ideal motive and the legal buttressing that the Americans and the Coalition were looking for. The BBC report contends, 'Authority to use force against Iraq exists from the combined effect of resolution 678, 687, and 1441. The Security Council also decided that if Iraq failed at any time to comply with and cooperate fully with the implementation of 1441, that would constitute a further material breach'.[37]

The American intervention too has been assailed as being criminal for

> the denizen's vocation of day-to-day drudgery when the UNSC and the Americans slapped sanctions on the Baghdad Regime. It can be deliberated in this manner too. One can delve inside the politics of the sanctions too. The question that has been raised by the 'Free Press' and the 'left media conglomerates' happens to be that of the following order. The question was that were the sanctions required to cripple the Saddam Hussein Regime to submission. David Rieff wrote in the *New York Times*, 'Others argue that the fundamental reason Iraq is in such terrible shape, is not Hussein's brutality but rather the comprehensive regime of economic sanctions that the United Nations Security Council imposed on Iraq for almost 13 years, sharply restricting all foreign trade'.[38] He further wrote, 'It was these sanctions, they claim, that brought this once rich country to its knees. For many people, the sanctions on Iraq were one of the decade's great crimes, as appalling as Bosnia or Rwanda. Anger at the United States and Britain, the two principal architects of the policy, often ran 'red hot'.[39]

It is quite a hypocritical situation to adhere to when on one hand the left-liberal bias in the Global Media challenges the tenability of the American intervention in Iraq while, on the flip side of it, rejects the impact of the economic sanctions on Iraq, which is an act far removed from the grime of a full-fledged military action. Sanctions cause infirmities for the local populace but the grime and the collateral damage associated with any all-out and direct military action with 'boots on the ground' can be evaded quite handsomely with the slapping of sanctions on recalcitrant nation states such as Iraq under the Saddam Hussein Regime. Sanctions are a softer and a humane way out of the carcass of direct military options. War must not be a perennial way out.

Nancy D Soberberg, of the National Security Council, expressed her disgruntlement over the insanity and inappropriateness of the anti-sanctions camp in the global firmament. As Rieff said in the *New York Times* report,

> Even today, Clinton-era American officials ranging from Madeleine K. Albright, the former secretary of state, and James P. Rubin, State Department spokesman under Albright, to Nancy E. Soderberg, then with the National Security Council, speak with anger and bitterness over the fervor of the anti-sanctions camp. As Soderberg put it to me, 'I could not give a speech anywhere in the U.S. without someone getting up and accusing me of being responsible for the deaths of 500,000 Iraqi children'.[40]

If that is the issue of death of the 5 lakh odd Iraqi children, then where can it be related to the sleeping death of the people in the Kurd villages. It was in the massacres such as the one of Halabja where thousands of Kurds slept one night in their homes while the bio-chemical weapons were sprayed over them by the Iraq Air Force. Most of the villagers never woke up after the bio-chemical attacks, and it is this side of the entire Iraqi picture that never comes to the fore on the lines of a 'perfect clean act Genocide'. Also, it can be argued that no voices pertaining to IHL and other norms of International Law have been incorporated as the standard literature on the war in Iraq.

Dursun Peksen writes in the context of the impacts of economic sanctions on recalcitrant nations in the *Journal of Peace Research*,

> Does economic coercion increase or decrease government respect for human rights in countries targeted with economic sanctions? If economic sanctions weaken the target regime's coercive capacity, human rights violations by the government should be less likely. If, on the contrary, sanctions fail to attenuate the coercive capacity of the target elites and create more economic difficulties and political violence among ordinary citizens, the government will likely commit more human rights violations. Focusing on competing views of why sanctions might improve or deteriorate human rights conditions, and there can be an empirical examination of the effect sanctions have on the physical integrity rights of citizens in target countries.[41]

Thus, the article posits that sanctions are unwanted and cannot amount to a full-fledged solution to the problem of war in rogue nation states.

An argument can be extended in the favour of sanctions too. Michael Spagat writes in the *Pacific Standard*,

> A few months later, in August 1996, Osama bin Laden cited the deaths of 600,000 Iraqi children in a fatwa declaring war against the U.S. 'More than 600,000 Iraqi children have died due to lack of food and medicine and as a result of the unjustifiable aggression (sanction) imposed on Iraq and its nation', he said. 'The children of Iraq are our children. You, the USA, together with the Saudi regime are responsible for the shedding of the blood of these innocent children'.[42]

Thus, the statements of personages such as the slain Al Qaeda chieftain cannot be taken as an authentic estimate of the resulting grime in Iraq premised upon the extended terror's notion of 'humanism'.

The writer in the *Pacific Standard* further writes, 'The claim that sanctions killed hundreds of thousands of Iraqi children originated in a 1995 letter to *The Lancet* which, in turn, was based on a Baghdad survey done by Sarah Zaidi and colleagues. When Zaidi failed to confirm quite a few of the reported deaths in these follow-up interviews, she retracted her results'.[43] It can be stressed that nobody denies that the slapping of sanctions on developing nations with a globally inimical regime leads to penury for the local population. Still, the genocidal proportions and the 'humanitarian disaster avatar' of the consequences of sanctions, is, too much of a task to digest and is a tale that attempts to eulogize Saddam Hussein and imparts a halo-like status to the Iraqi Dictator, who finally was captured from rat/hell-hole near Baghdad after his Regime's entire structure collapsed, akin to Adolf Hitler in the city dungeon of Berlin many years back. So much so for the American interventionism and alacrity at poking its nose in others' matters!!!!!!!!!!!!!!!

NOTES

1. McLuhan, Marshall, *Understanding Media: The Extensions of Men*, New York : McGraw-Hill Publications, 2003, pp. 10–20.
2. 'How Media Coverage has changed in Recent Times'. http://www.scribd.com/doc/191652/glossary. Accessed 8 May 2017.
3. 'Importance of Free, Independent Press, Role of Journalists in Iraq War'. http://www.un.org/News/Press/docs/2003/pi1480.doc.htm. Accessed 10 May 2017.
4. Bellamy, Christopher, *Expert Witness: A Defense Correspondent's Gulf War, 1990-91*, New York: Brassey's Publications, 1992, p. 252.
5. Ibid.
6. Ibid.
7. http://www.newamericancentury.org/. Accessed 1 September 2007.
8. *Project for the New American Century*. http://www.newamericancentury.org/. Accessed 4 September 2007. It is a non-profit educational organization dedicated to a few fundamental propositions: that American leadership is good both for America and for the world, and that such leadership requires military strength, diplomatic energy and commitment to moral principle.
9. Butler, Judith, 'Photography, War and Outrage', *Modern Language Association*, 1, 2003, pp. 822–827.
10. Carlson, Timothy and Bill Katvosky, *Embedded: The Media At War in Iraq: An Oral History*, Cincinnati: Lyons Press, 2004, pp. 60–80.
11. Moos, Julie M. 'Journalists Die in Iraq', http://poynter.org/content/content_view.asp?id = 28739. Accessed 10 December 2007,
12. Ibid.
13. The National Security Archive, 'The Interrogation Documents: Debating U.S. Policy and Methods', 14 July 2004 www.commondreams.org. Accessed 7 May 2009,
14. United States Department of Defense. 'Victoria Clarke on The Embedded Process', News

Transcript, Presenter: Victoria Clarke, ASD. http://media.leeds.ac.uk/papers/vp0139b9.html.

15. Soros, George, 'The Bubble of American Supremacy', *The Atlantic*, Boston, 2 December 2003.
16. 'The US and the North Korean Peninsula', http://usinfo.state.gov/eap/east_asia_pacific/north_korea.html.
17. An excerpt, 'Despite delays in shutting down a North Korean nuclear facility at the center of an agreement reached in the Six-Party Talks, lead U.S. envoy Christopher Hill believes the February 13 plan still can be implemented as planned. "We continue to believe that the best way to achieve denuclearization is to move step-by-step," Hill, the Assistant secretary of state for East Asian and Pacific affairs'.
18. Pillar, Paul R., 'Intelligence and US Foreign Policy: Iraq, 9/11 and Misguided Reform', Columbia University Press, 2014, pp. 155–157.
19. Ibid., p. 148.
20. Military intelligence official quoted in Thomas E. Ricks' *Fiasco: The American Military Adventure in Iraq*, New York: Penguin, 2006, p. 51.
21. Secretary of Defense Donald H. Rumsfeld, Statement to the US Senate, Armed Services Committee, 107th Congress, 2nd Session, 19 September 2002.
22. Judith Miller, *The New York Times*, February 2003.
23. Owen, Lord David, 'A Clinician's Caution: Rhetoric and Reality', in *Preventive Diplomacy: Stopping Wars Before They Start*, Kevin M Cahill (ed.), New York: Routledge, 2000, pp. 5–10.
24. Ibid., p. 220.
25. Article 35, UN Charter.
26. Weiner, Tim, 'US Long View on Iraq: View on Iraq: Patience is Containing the Ever deadlier Hussein', *The New York Times*, 3 January 1999.
27. 'Iraq War was Illegal and Breached U N Charter', *The Guardian*, 16 September 2004.
28. Ibid.
29. United Nations Security Council Resolution 1441 (2002), Adopted by the Security Council at its 4644th meeting on 8 November 2002.
30. Ibid.
31. Ibid.
32. 'UN Role in Iraq', https://www.globalpolicy.org/political-issues-in-iraq/un-role-in-iraq.html. Accessed 10 May 2017.
33. Ibid.
34. British Broadcasting Corporation, 'Fact Check: Was the Iraq War Legal?' http://news.bbc.co.uk/2/hi/uk_news/politics/vote_2005/issues/4492443.stm. Accessed 10 May 2017.
35. Ibid.
36. Ibid.
37. Ibid.
38. Rieff, David, 'Were sanctions Right?' *The New York Times*, 27 July 2003.
39. Ibid.
40. Ibid.
41. Pecksen, Dursen, 'Better or Worse? The Effects of Economic Sanctions on Human Rights', *Journal of Peace Research*, 46(1), 2009, pp. 59–77.
42. Spagat, Michael, 'The Iraq Sanctions Myth', *Pacific Standard*, 27 April 2013.
43. Ibid.

9

Syria Through the Ides of Scylla and Charybdis

SYRIA is, too, bedevilled by the ides of regional conflict and the satanic vicissitudes of civil war. I call it Satanic as once upon a time a nation perched atop the cusp of modernity has been forced to part with millions of its population worth the salt of the nation with the context of besieged cities, destroyed town malls and avenues. This gargantuan cascade of inhuman smatterings calls for global attention that they have been able to attract but with little impact upon the way, diplomacy has to be invented for being kosher to the ides of times in the nation state of Syria. Syria is now the biggest humani tarion crisis, which, the world has ever seen.

The consequences and the genocidal proportion of the civilian torment can be gauged from the idiom of twin incidents in the contemporary context of the Syrian nation. In one specific imagery, one can imagine a pool party that is taking place in a five-star revelry hotel in Damascus, where-in, the distant shots of gunfire can be heard in the dark night. In the similar context, the women in leotards and swimsuits with men of their choice frolic around near the swimming pool with the military brass band playing in the background.

The author could have felt the feel of unease and insecurity and incertitude in the air in the pool party mandarins, as, some of them declare this outing to be their last gathering in the capital. Most of the families have contacted their families and relatives in the United States and other Western nations and are about to be teleported to safe havens in the United States and other Western stations. The eerie bursts of gun fire and rocket sounds sound the final death knell of the scenario in Damascus that not in a distant past before 2011 used to be a favourite tourist destination for travellers from across the far-off corners of the international system.

In another related development, a lady is all determined to pass her days in a cage which is 8 feet in height and 5 feet in breadth. The lady was part of the rebel movement with the Al-Nusra and other Islamic fronts with touches and brushes with the Islamic State. She used to write pamphlets and used to attend the protest rallies and secret hideout meetings of the rebel groups. One fine day, Bashar al-Assad's secret police got the air of her activities and machinations as they put it, and they raided her home where her parents and family members were pushed aside and she was forced to live with other 'pigeons' in the casket-like cages for a few years.

When she was rescued by the humanitarian agencies a few years back, then, she had stopped talking and spoke only in sign language. She wrote and told that she was initially repeatedly raped and was incarcerated in a cage merely a foot bigger than her size. She had to stay there for the whole day and she was freed to only freshen up herself. When she was rescued, she could not stay alone as she had completely lost confidence in herself. She held a mass communication degree from one of the universities of Damascus, and earlier on, as a free lady with the non-violent rebels, ran errands for the rebel groups.

Thus, the errands of the Bashar al-Assad Regime happen to be supported by the Russians and the 'Shia Iran' while this cold-war confabulation is pitted against the rebel groups, comprising the Al-Nusra group, which are on the other side of the fence in a larger war on terror, which gets its confrontation gifted as a set piece of the larger conflict in West Asia. Thus, the Americans here come under the critical scanner because of a want of 'boots on the ground' and a want of military intervention in Syria, when the conditions reflecting the humanitarian excesses by the Bashar Regime called for an American intervention, and much more should have been on the cards than a regime change as achieved in Libya. Syria was another test case for President Obama's ruling denomination, but his entreaties to Iran in the context of the Joint Comprehensive Plan of Action nuclear deal and his disinterest to intervene in Syria after the criticism of Iraq reflected a larger American withdrawal mentality from its global responsibilities. David Sanger writes in his work, *The Inheritance*,

> The Iranians tried to explain away the centrifuges. As they liked to point out to anyone who would listen, the Japanese had them, as did many non-nuclear states in Europe, and no one was complaining about their nuclear programme. To the rest of the World, that was beside the point: Iran had hidden its activities for seventeen years disqualifying them from ordinary treatment. United States may never know when the Iranians may decide to take the leap to a civilian nuclear programe to a weapon. As along as the Mullahs keep that uncertainty alive, they will survive, otherwise not.[1]

The West Asian policy as inherited by President Obama had its challenges and the manner in which President Obama sided with Iran led to the falling political fortunes of the Democrats in the lead-up to the elections starring Donald Trump. It was Donald Trump who targeted Obama and the larger Democrats with the blame that the larger American policy in West Asia, including the hot spots of Syria, Iraq, Israel and other nations, had come a cropper and it portrayed a weakened and disinterested America that was bolstered by Trump's clarion call of 'America First'. The revalidation and the resuscitation of the American Dream had to become the order of the day and which is what President Trump has initiated with the blast of the 'mother of all bombs', or MOAB, on the Af–Pak border and the firing of screaming missiles in Syria and Yemen. Thus, despite Trump's declaration of making America make good its retreat, he did not follow the 'silent-stratagem' of President Obama vis-à-vis West Asia and Syria. And, now in December 2018, the larger segment of the American troops has been withdrawn from Syria which is earning a great deal of ire for President Trump and even from his own co mate Republicans, as, the entire world looks forward to a "Forward Policy" on the part of United States and not a genre of diplomatic and meek isolationism.

Thus, the American intervention was limited to military advisors along with maintaining a BoP of diplomacy with the nation state play-actors in West Asia. America was missing in action for the first time while a conflict, a simple civil war, metamorphosed gradually into a humanitarian disaster. It's no criticism of the United States, but it all amounts to the theme that the US was more than conspicuous by its presence.

America has always had the penchant and the inclination to intervene despite the criticism and the strategic and diplomatic hoopla attached to its ministrations. But, America was not to be found militating against the

Damascus regime of Bashar al-Assad. There was one palpable interest that confronting the Government in Syria would have meant a direct confrontation with Iran and Russia with its nationalistic and gung-ho Czar, Vladimir Putin playing a role even in the 2017 American Elections. Still what America does and intermeshes comes with an inherent cost as related to by the British Prime Minister, Winston Churchill.

Winston Churchill contends in his work, *My Early Life*, in 1930, as reproduced by David Sanger,

> Let us learn our lessons. Never, never, never believe that any war will be smooth and easy or that anyone who embarks on that strange voyage can measure the tides and hurricanes that he will encounter. The Statesman who yields to war fever must realize that once the signal is given, he is no longer the master of the policy but the slave of the unforeseeable and uncontrollable events. Antiquated war offices, weak, incompetent or arrogant Commanders, untrustworthy allies, hostile neutrals, malignant Fortune, ugly surprises, awful miscalculations—all take their seats at the Council Board on the morrow of a declaration of war.[2]

Maybe President Obama was no President Bush and chose to align with what Winston Churchill had to impart as a nugget to the Statesman of the future of the Brave New World. But despite his adherence to the ideals of the American Founding Fathers amounting to 'No Entangling Alliances', President Trump has done a volte-face, with his campaign trail Foreign Policy Byte that declared that America will not get involved in far-off lands and their civil and internecine disputes. But, as with great power comes great responsibility, the US is expected to take upon itself the mantle of the larger international system. Also, Syria happens to be one case in point, where-in, a more well-pronounced and well-entangled web of an intervention has to be on the anvil if the international responsibility of being the benign regulator, has, to be achieved and deftly realised.

Regulate, Yes, America should in Syria. Syria remains at a strategic cusp and is perched upon a cataclysmic and catastrophic calamity with the mass exodus of Syrian refugees leaving for the Eastern European blocks of Belgium, Yugoslavia, Germany and other nations. The entire ruckus around the refuge crisis in Europe is related to the threat of Jihadi Terrorism and the threat of mass influx of unidentified aliens.The appellation of 'I am a Syrian Refugee' is going to be identified as part of the larger plight of Syria and the European receptacles. The UNSC has also expressed its concern about the refugee crisis in Syria along with the condition of women and children as part of the brewing humanitarian crisis in a besieged Syria.

UN Resolution 2336 resolved by the UNSC refers to the fact of the ongoing civil war in Syria. The resolution reflects the concern of the international community and the extraneous nations such as Turkey and Russia. The UNSC clamour is also generally aimed at attaining a ceasefire in the battleground of Syria between the governmental regime and the various other warring factions. As one delves inside the text of the UNSC Resolution 2336, one can gauge the international concern about the carnage in Syria. Some of the sections run as such,

> Noting with appreciation the mediation efforts undertaken by the Russian Federation and the Republic of Turkey to facilitate the establishment of a ceasefire in the Syrian Arab Republic, Reiterating its call on the parties to allow humanitarian agencies rapid, safe and unhindered access throughout Syria, as provided for in its relevant resolutions,[3] Reiterating that the only sustainable solution to the current crisis in the Syrian Arab Republic is through an inclusive and Syrian-led political process based on the Geneva Communiqué of 30 June 2012 as endorsed by resolution 2118 (2013), its resolutions 2254 (2015) and 2268 (2016) and relevant statements of the International Syria Support Group.[4] Welcomes and supports the efforts by Russia and Turkey to end violence in Syria and jump start a political process, and takes note of the documents issued by Russia and Turkey in this regard (S/2016/1133).[5]

The entire effort led by the United States and Russia happens to be that of subscribing to the political process in the nation state of Syria with an inclusion of a Syria-led political process that is one of the core concerns of the mandarins in the United Nations along with the negotiating parties in Syria. The Secretary General, too, has written reports on the humanitarian situation in Syria. One such report was published in March, 2017. The key themes of the Report by the Secretary General can be referred to here as part of these deliberations. The key themes run as thus,

> Despite the ceasefire that has been in effect since 30 December 2016, continued fighting in multiple areas around the country resulted in further civilian deaths and injury as well as destruction of civilian

> infrastructure.[6] Two inter-agency convoys proceeded in February, reaching 191,500 people. On 5 February, a joint United Nations/ International Committee of the Red Cross/Syrian Arab Red Crescent convoy reached Talbisah, and, on 12 February, another such joint convoy reached 107,500 beneficiaries in Rastan. On 20 February, after a convoy destined for War was forced to turn back, trucks were diverted, aid was taken and drivers were abused.[7] The situation in eastern Ghouta (Rif Dimashq), where hundreds of thousands of people are being besieged in a number of towns and surrounding rural areas, conditions deteriorated throughout the month amid reports of shelling, air strikes and ground.[8]

Keeping in view the humanitarian situation in the state of Syria, it becomes all the more pertinent that the great power interventions and mediation can be inculcated as part of the ceasefire and other negotiations on Syria. The Report also includes an estimate of the total number of displaced population till early 2017 along with zeroing upon the infrastructure damage including the damage to bridges and the accessibility of the humanitarian convoys in the troubled spots in Syria. The issue of the Report is also about the collateral damage being inflicted by the Bashar al-Assad Regime in Syria as nearly the entire terrain of warfare includes the zones of urban warfare.

The other facet of the matter is that over the Syrian quagmire, the great powers of the order of the United States and Russia are nearly at loggerheads and some of the IR observers have declared the advent of 'New Cold War' under the ambit of the Syrian civil war. It has been reported in the context of the Syrian Civil War,

> A United Nations Security Council resolution condemning the reported use of chemical weapons in Syria and demanding access for investigators failed Wednesday because of a Russian veto. It is the eighth time Russia has vetoed a resolution on Syria since the start of the country's civil war in 2011. Following the vote, Russia's envoy to the U.N. said the 'doomed draft' had 'appointed the guilty party prior to the investigation'. China, another permanent member of the Security Council, abstained from the vote. Ethiopia, a non-permanent member, also abstained. Bolivia and Kazakhstan, both non-permanent members, voted against the draft.[9]

Thus, diplomatic strivings were turned on by the Russians in order to curtail the American tinkering in the civil war. Also, the Russians have always blocked the UNSC Resolutions that hint at the culpability of the Bashar al-Assad

Regime. Thus, an internecine and regionally destabilizing narrative in the region has been festooned by the Syrian regime by the support and succour of the partisan Vladimr Putin's regime, though with the advent of President Trump, the idea of an American confrontation with Russia has receded with the Americans, too, searching for a regional ally in the form of Premier Vladimir Putin. The connections that have surfaced in the ambit of the relationship between the United States and Russia, have, already made President Trump scale difficult terrains but the new-found policy of President Trump to wed Moscow with the strategic, political and diplomatic purposes of Vladimir Putin, might preclude a confrontation over Syria.

Let's look at the official standpoint that the Americans have in the context of Syria. The US Congress passed Resolution 856 in the 113th Congress. The Congressional resolution was titled as 'To Foster Stability in Syria and for other purposes'. Some of the sections of the Congressional Resolution are reproduced here that shed eminent light on the scenario in Syria. The preliminary sections shed eminent light,

> Since mass peaceful demonstrations started in Syria on March 15, 2011, the Government of Syria, led by President Bashar al-Assad, has responded by committing human rights abuses and launching a violent crackdown that has claimed an estimated 70,000 lives and degenerated into a civil war.[10] The civil war has caused a humanitarian crisis. According to the United Nations, there are more than 1,400,000 Syrian refugees registered in Lebanon, Turkey, Jordan, Egypt, Iraq and more than 2,600,000 Syrian refugees displaced within the country.[11]

Thus, the Congressional Resolution pinpoints at the gathering storm with humanitarian proportions that according to the understanding of the American lawmakers sets the bail on President Bashar al-Assad's policies. House Resolution (HR) 233 too pinpoints towards the Syrian quagmire. The relevant sections of the HR Resolution read as such, 'Expressing the sense of the House of Representatives concerning the ongoing conflict in Syria and the urgent need for the Syrian Opposition Coalition and local coordinating committees in Syria to assume the responsibilities of governance including the establishment of institutions of transitional justice, and to guarantee the rights of all Syria's people, regardless of ethnic or religious affiliation'.[12]

The HR Resolution further reads,

> Whereas the 40-year history of undemocratic, repressive leadership

> under the regime of Bashar al Assad and his father Hafez al Assad has eroded civil society, debilitated the capacity for self government, and undermined confidence in the rule of law in Syria; Where as the Syrian opposition, though lacking comprehensive and coordinated assistance from the international community, and suffering constant attacks by the Assad regime, has succeeded in establishing effective self-government in significant sections of the country and is developing a capacity to exercise responsible authority and deliver essential services.[13]

Thus, the American standpoint is amply reflected in the Syrian crisis and the US lawmakers attempt to cobble together a Governing edifice while the conflict smoulders down in Syria. The Congressional Resolution also cites the historical antiquities of regimental oppression and non-fulfilment of justice to the Syrian population even under the suzerainty of Hafez al-Assad, Bashar al-Assad's father, who too blazed a trail of exploitative policies over his own hoi polloi/ the citizens of Syria.

The other prominent concern of the US administration and the legislature has been the transition of Syria through a process of peace along with the ushering in of democracy in the besieged nation state. Democratic transition is largely the key corpus of the fundamentals of US foreign policy with the Americans kow-towing along with the value-laden approach and strategic perch of America as the joker player, an international peace broker and largesse mediator. One of the Congressional Resolutions reads thus,

> In December 2011, the Government of Syria agreed to allow an Arab League observer group into the country to assess the humanitarian and political situation on the ground. However, on January 28, 2012, the League officially ended its observer mission, citing escalating violence and the intransigence of the Assad regime. In February 2012, the group Friends of the Syrian People met in Tunis and issued a declaration demanding, among other things, that the Syrian regime "allow free and unimpeded access by the United Nations and humanitarian agencies to carry out a full assessment of needs.[14]

The snide and now very clearly delineated references to the brewing humanitarian crisis in Syria, along with deliberations on the post-2011 excesses of the Bashar al-Assad Regime, highlight the need to regulate and mediate in the crisis-ridden imbroglio in the Syrian State with adequate references to the astutely repressive policies of the Regime even 30 to 40 years back in the past. Then, the consequential support of the Russian Government to the Bashar al-

Assad Regime and the antecedent of the Iranian backing accentuate the tensions in the region every now and then. It is this kind of the directionless advancement of the negotiations on Syria that has bolstered the hands of detrimental outfits such as the Islamic State.

President Donald Trump has eschewed the silent approach policy towards Syria, and the American establishment carried out strikes on Syria. The Brookings Institution informs us,

> It must also have dawned on President Trump this week that his words and actions matter and were not incidental to the crisis. Trump had repeatedly said he would not try to remove Assad, that he would not prioritize human rights, that his singular focus was ISIS, and that he would not act where American interests were not directly threatened. It would be America First.[15]

Still, President Trump after coming to the power perch in the White House shifted his policy vision when he ordered military strikes on Syria, thus reversing the Withdrawal policy paradigm of his campaign trail policy comprehension on West Asia and Syria in particular. Apart from the inhuman incident of a Syrian kid Aylan Kurdi being washed up on the beach, the gory nature and objective of the Syrian chemical attacks on the commoners has led to the idiom that Trump's condemning the atrocity was both, genuine, sincere and kosher. President Trump was the personage during the election trail who attacked president Obama on his silent and wait-and-watch policy in Syria that belittled the pelf and the strategic expanse of the United States as a powerful Regulator nation. President's Trump move on Syria with the missile strikes is a just and bold move that differentiates him from the lax approach of President Obama. Still, the December, 2018 decision of the White House to withdraw a larger part of the American contingent from Syria leaves the entire region in the lurch in a region which might become sans a net security provider and an astute balancer.

Micah Zenko writes in *Foreign Policy* that the missile take on Syria occurred without any Congressional consent. But it also needs to be stressed that the same Congressional lawmakers have unearthed a plethora of blame to be placed on President Bashar al-Assad who has been high-handed in governing his people. Zenko writes,

> In the summer of 2014, the Obama administration initiated another war of choice in the Middle East. The intervention in Iraq had two

> stated objectives: On Thursday, President Donald Trump slid further down this same intervention slope by authorizing the attack of a Syrian military airfield in Homs with 59 cruise missiles. According to a Pentagon news release, the military objective was not to harm Russian or Syrian forces, but to damage 'aircraft, hardened aircraft shelters, petroleum and logistical storage, ammunition supply bunkers, air defense systems, and radars' saving Yazidis at risk of genocide and defeating the Islamic State.[16]

Thus, despite the soft-gloved treatment of the West Asian and the Syrian milieu, President Trump returned with a penchant for bamboozling the American adversaries in Syria that happened to be the personages such as Bashar al-Assad. In a manner, the American gaffe as perceived during the times of President Obama was sought to be redone with President Trump 'missiling' Syria, its Air Force and chemical weapons dumps. President Trump has also created his anti-immigration drive that militates against the interests of several Moslem nations especially Syria, as these nations are present in the 'No entry' list of President Trump. Thus, I would perceive the Trumpian policy not as a reflection of American xenophobia, but, a kind of securitization of the homeland that separates out certain nations and its populations from seeking refuge and further settlement in America. America with its own list of undocumented aliens, mainly hailing from South America and South Asia, amounts to an alarming number of 12 odd million people, that, in itself requires intervention by the Washington Administration.

We can have a look at the idea that what is Trump's Syria Policy? First of all, it's all about being aggressive with avoidance of a direct military intervention in the nation's territory. Still, some of the observers of the West Asian politics have opined that missile attacks on Syrian military and Air Force Depots amount to the initiation of a new war and a novae American intervention and engagement. The missile attacks on Syria are not being perceived as a singular acts of aggression against the Islamic State, but, it is being perceived as a precursor element in the large spate of incidents and policy decisions to follow. It's a singular step in a trail of events to follow:

> David Graham writes in the *Atlantic*, 'President Trump himself has been uncharacteristically quiet about why and how he decided to order airstrikes against a target in Syria, and for what they indicate about U.S. policy toward Syrian President Bashar al-Assad going forward'.[17] Thus, despite prognostications from the Fourth Estate and other

> academic and policy observations, the actual trail and the framework of the policy to emerge can be earmarked for a future policy deliberation on the United States of America. The same author highlighted the now-transformed approach of the United States that is a maximalist stance on Syria and other West Asian matters. He wrote about the need for a change in the Russian stance about the Syrian civil war. He wrote in the *Atlantic*, Tillerson surprised some observers when, hours before his flight to Moscow, he said in Lucca, Italy, 'We rededicate ourselves to holding to account any and all who commit crimes against the innocents anywhere in the world'. Tillerson also said Russia had to choose between working with the West or with Assad, 'which we believe is not going to serve Russia's interests in the longer term'. By promising to go after those commit 'any and all' crimes, he seemed to be suggesting an aggressively interventionist stance—a maximalist vision of America as the world's policeman.[18]

Still, America seemingly sticks to the viewpoint that nations ought not to violate international agreements and if they do so then they should be prepared for action by the 'Justice League' along with recrimination from the myriad global bodies. In the Syrian context, it has been a policy formulation of the American dispensation that the United States feared a humanitarian crisis in Syria that had materialized, and apart from that, a political process as part of a transitory phase ought to be the chief characteristic approach of the negotiators in Syria beyond mere talks for a 'ceasefire'.

People are discussing with interest, President Donald Trump's change of heart on Syria, that is, the larger Syria Policy. A CNN report highlights the fact,

> President Donald Trump's decision to authorize a missile strike against a Syrian air base Thursday night signals a major break not only with the Obama administration but also with past statements made by the President himself. Fifty Tomahawk missiles were fired at the air base from which the chemical attacks against Syrian civilians were launched earlier this week and left more than 70 people dead. 'It is in the vital national security interests of America to prevent and deter the spread and use of deadly chemical weapons', Trump said in a statement from his Mar-a-Lagao estate.[19]

The notion that seems to have fired the American people, is the realization that Bashar al-Assad chokes his own people and does the needful to hurt the interests of the helpless and uncared for. Thus, the decision to 'missile' Syria marks a new reversal for the American President.

One can delve inside the consequences of the Staffan De Mistura's diplomatic efforts too in the context of Syria. The Syrian talks in Geneva in March 2017 have ended with a clear agenda on the anvil. Though the talks have crumbled in the light of the collapsing status of the ceasefire, the negotiations for 'restoring Syria' have been going on strong and in an upbeat manner. Dylan Collins informs in Al Jazeera, that talks are here to stay and the agreement would revolve around the UNSC Resolution 2254 with the issues of constitution formation and ascertaining governance for the commoners, being the mainstay part of a solution to the Syrian quagmire.[20] Collins writes, 'It is now clear to everyone that we are here to implement the Security Council resolution 2254, and that is beyond dispute. Resolution 2254, adopted by the council in 2015, lays the foundations for a political transition—the opposition's central goal—based on three subjects, or "baskets": accountable governance, a new constitution and UN-supervised elections within 18 months'.[21] Thus, a political process akin to the American standpoint is being envisaged by the interlocutors on Syria that is a positive fall-out of the talks to stymie the further proliferation of the conflict. The American standpoint provides the icing on the cake with involving the final erosion of the strength and the pelf of the Islamic State as one of the objectives of the global intervention in Syria. The word 'terror' also gets a clear mention in the talks that have been continued to end the rut that Syria finds itself in, despite the myriad Islamic factions and their 'grouplets' also doing the equally frequent rounds in the tricky Syrian cesspool. Now, President Donald Trump in 2019 has decided to withdraw from Syria which might render the region unstable entangles with more challenges.

NOTES

1. Sanger, David E., *The Inheritance: The World Obama Confronts and the Challenges to American Power*, London: Bantam Press, 2009, pp. 12–30.
2. Ibid., Winston Churchill, 'My Early Life', 1930, pp. 1–5.
3. United Nations Security Council Resolution No. 2336 (2016). Adopted by the Security Council at its 7855th meeting, on 31 December 2016.
4. Ibid.
5. Ibid.
6. United Nations Security Council, Report of the UN Secretary General on 22 March 2017. http://www.securitycouncilreport.org/atf/cf/%7B65BFCF9B-6D27-4E9C-8CD3-CF6E4FF96FF9%7D/s_2017_244.pdf. Accessed 10 May 2017.

7. Ibid.
8. Ibid.
9. Shelbourne, Mallory, 'Russia Blocks UN Resolution on Syria'. http://thehill.com/policy/international/un-treaties/328540-un-security-council-fails-to-pass-resolution-to-investigate. Accessed 10 May 2017.
10. US Congress Resolution No. 856, 113th Congress, Ist Session.
11. Ibid.
12. House of Representatives Resolution No. 233, 113rd Congress, 1st Session on Syria.
13. Ibid.
14. United States Congress, US Senate Resolution No. 617, 'To Provide humanitarian Assistance and Support a Democratic Transition in Syria and For Other Purposes'.
15. Wright, Thomas, 'What the Syria Strikes tell us about Trump's Foreign Policy'. https://www.brookings.edu/blog/order-from-chaos/2017/04/07/what-the-syria-strikes-tell-us-about-trumps-foreign-policy/. Accessed 19 May 2017.
16. Zenko, Micah, 'Trump's Humanitarian Intervention in Syria is Just Getting Started', *Foreign Policy*, 9 April 2017.
17. Graham, David, 'What is Trump's Syria Policy?' *The Atlantic*, 11 April 2017.
18. Ibid.
19. CNN Report by Chris Cillizza, 'Trump Change of Heart on Syria', CNN Editor-at-Large, http://edition.cnn.com/2017/04/06/politics/trump-syria-foreign-policy/index.html. Accessed 19 May 2017.
20. Collins, Dylan, 'De Mistura: Syria Talks in Geneva End with Clear Agenda', 4 March 2017, Al Jazeera Report.
21. Ibid.

10

Trump's Internationalism and Interventionism: A Tour de Force by America

PRESIDENT Donald Trump has lot to preach and practicalize both in the domestic domain and in the international context. The talk about Trump elevates because it's all embedded in the larger contemporary context of the international system. President Trump can make for an interesting case study in psychological studies as the entire persona of the American President bespeaks of surprises, shocking aggression and if one would disparage like his critics, the ides of whims, idiosyncrasies and piquant posturing. The author would hate to agree with the critics of President Donald Trump as akin to the former President Barrack Obama, Trump invented his credo of 'bravado policy' with ecclesiastical, political and diplomatic aplomb.

He attempted to do work for the blue-collar worker and the unemployment-ridden commoners that were left bereft of opportunities in the larger American frame. President Donald Trump in the author's perception lives and intends to make the hoi polloi, the next-door war veteran, the next door entrepreneur live the American Dream with the quintessential America-First approach.

President Donald Trump's rise is all about the efficacy and the rejuvenation of the grandiloquent American Dream and his rise to the 'power perch' is a testament to the serendipitous incident in the political history of the United States of America. The man just cannot take hands on, the belittlement and the disparaging of his homeland and the contrails of Blue, Red and White fliers need to fly high for him when he alights on a rostrum to deliver his speech. All the glitz, canny chutzpah and the paraphernalia are there for the buntings and it's not all about beatific and consumerist fanfare, but largely and completely about what the new President wants America to achieve with its trail of 'believing hoi polloi'. The electorate have legally sent him to become the most powerful man in the international comity of nation states or on the face of the larger Earth. He is an Super-Earthling par excellence.

President Donald Trump was known to be the withdrawal crusader for American interventions abroad. But, it has been cheekily observed by IR and American commentators that the campaign trail byte of asking America to live behind its 'Atlantic and Pacific moats' is no longer the contemporary credo of the American policy context. Rather, the expansiveness and accentuating of the American domain, footprint and perch in the global comity of nations as denizens have been gradually betrothed as the new policy paradigm in America. Though America longingly intends to make the NATO and other allied nations pay for the American security umbrella, still, the urge and the penchant for 'Regally Regulating' the New World order in an age of multipolarity and multiple power centres comes with a cost. America is at risk of being disparaged and lampooned as a Messiah forcing its 'do-gooder instincts and philanthropy' at the litany of nation states. But, the positivity about US is also not sheer coincidence.

The million-dollar question is that can the world live up and match the footsteps of President Trump as he 'Trumps Up' the ante for the rollercoaster ride with the renewed vigour of American leadership in a post-recession world?That's what we intend to investigate with President Trump closing the 'Fortress's Gates' with his anti-immigration policy (which was always in the offing with the previous Administrations too), his interventions in the Korean Peninsula and the attitude in the South China Seas along with mollycoddling with Taiwan in the neighbourhood of the People's Republic of China. Thus, a great trail of event-filled Global Politics is on the offing with the resurfacing of a 'New World Order Interventionism' of America, but, with an all-encompassing amalgamative zeal.

The clarion call that President Donald Trump has given to the larger masses and the international community by walking out of the Paris Climate Accord, is, a kind of interventionism that reeks of a sequestration and isolation (withdrawal) from the global high seat of negotiations and power.[1] President Trump has also sought a new injunction from one of the Circuit Courts in the United States, where-in the limitations on the ban on seven moslem nations for migration have been asked to be rescinded.[2] Thus, the clarion call has received a new well-defined byte this time around, 'I represent the People of Pittsburgh, not Paris', which is something President Donald Trump echoed in the city of Pittsburgh that has seen the rise and fall of the industrial rust and coal belt. It is not sheer populism that we are referring to here, but the idiom of American reflexivism and progression into a novae world order, as, President Trump comprehends it to be. Still, how can the American dictum of the American Dream and the, notion of, 'America first' be achieved by the American exit from the Climate Change Accord, remains to be seen in a globally functional manner.

Varghese K George reports for the national daily, *The Hindu*,

> Carbon Reduction targets that the US set under the Paris Accord aimed at reducing emissions by 26%-28% in a decade. The United States has stopped contributing to the Green Climate Fund (GCF) set up under the Paris Climate Agreement to support developing nations meet their requirements. The Obama Administration had committed 3 billion dollars for the Fund out of which only a quantum of one billion dollars has been transferred to the Green Climate Fund.[3]

This can be perceived as a decision to mark out the recalcitrant strain of the American President and the American establishment. Now, the responsibility to meander across the slew of climate action negotiations lies with the European Union under the leadership of nations such as Germany, Italy, France and the Chinese nation with India too coming the way of these nations to spawn a 'climate proactive' platform in order to reinvent the idea of Collective Climate Action, once America turns truant.

The American idea to exit the Paris Accord might be an offering in disguise as some of the observers have pointed out that its much worse than Trump remaining in the Pact's frame and narrowing down its pledge as an individual nation. This might have gone down with some of the developing nations in such a manner that some of them might have too walked out of the Paris Climate Agreement. This is a forgone possibility and an exercise to place the entire blame on the American negotiating side. President Donald Trump has, too, called for a renegotiation of the Paris Climate Agreement that none of the developing nations have agreed to. It can also be ascribed that China is the largest polluter in the larger international system, followed by the United States and India.

Still, United States being the ideational 'regulator high seat' of the global polity, trade and commerce, President Trump would have done well to stay put in the Paris Climate Agreement. The historical theme of the Paris plan would involve that around 195 nations signed the accord in December 2015, while, it was ratified in December 2016, but, when the shove had to come to a push, then at that crucial juncture, President Donald Trump decided to move out of the crucial accord.

President Donald Trump and How New Delhi Perceives the Juggernaut

Historically speaking, President Donald Trump came to the forefront through his 'America-First standpoint' in the context of the Presidential Election trail in the United States. As one harks back, one can ruminate over the prognosis that was being bandied around while he was yet to don the mantle of the American high seat of responsibility and power. Several forecasts were doing the rounds concerning the fate of the India–US relationship as part of the Trumpism and his projections vis-à-vis foreign policy, Asia and the nuclear relations.

Trump became the President-elect after a hard-fought campaign, tarnished by personal attacks. The Hillary-Trump rally showcased the American Dream of inclusiveness and national interest-directed foreign policy. The American Dream reflects all that is bright and ebullient about the United States. There is a spectacular element in the rubric of the American Dream, driven by the founding idols of constitutionalism, the rule of law and egalitarianism. US Presidential elections have been driven, much like any other electoral event, by the theatricals, histrionics and the ground reality of public opinion and media coverage.

Donald Trump has been everybody's pet peeve and a universal bête noire in the contemporary electoral times in the United States. The US is the land of stealth and partisan self, as far as the political legerdemain in the nation is concerned. The myriad nations, their political mandarins and the avid populations seem to be following the contemporary bytes on this heady trail of American elections. The issue that engaged the political pundits all across is that whether the official candidate and the diplomat par excellence, Hillary Clinton, will be crowned as the occupant of the pristine White House or will it be the paramount Regency of an iconoclast like Donald Trump, who, will transform himself from the steed of Presumptive Republican candidate to the most powerful personage on the face of the larger international system? It's a million-dollar question, and who emerges as the personage with the million-dollar arm is another quest worth undertaking.

The BBC has reported in one of its webcasts,

> A vote that would allow delegates to back a candidate of their choice was quashed when three states reportedly backed out. Some said the RNC sabotaged their efforts on purpose. The push was the last gasp for those who hope to see a different Republican candidate get the nomination. The nomination of Mr. Trump has been a source of conflict in the party.

The presumptive candidate is a nomenclature given to the consensually and democratically elected presidential candidate, but because of some of the popular remarks of Trump, voices were raised in the GOP too that cast a pall of gloom on the heady trail of his candidature. The capitalist veneer of Donald trump might not be an obstruction at all despite the shadow of the American and the global recession as the economy seems to be 'looking up' and 'the serpentine quest' for vocational opportunities as reported in mainstream Global Media is a gentle reminder that the US economy is steadily gaining back its girth and steed. Thus, the maverick capitalist streak of President Trump might be a façade to be toyed with stylistically. The vitriolic attacks on the American homeland have made only Donald Trump raise the issue of gun running and the intertwined fundamentalist angle added to the entire narrative. If it's a social ferment, then Donald Trump might be the 'Kosher' personage to oust the antagonist streak in the American firmament. He is the one and only to proclaim a 'War' against insidious terror and deranged attacks on innocent American denizens while other political personages including Hillary have trumpeted a balanced and safer line of an argument on the austere audacity of the attacks in South Carolina, San Bernardino, Dallas, etc. The Houser Speaker Paul Ryan is another latest entrant to the 'Presumptive' Trump bandwagon, as the American electorate might as well welcome the verbiage and the vivacious vitriol of Donald Trump as the President in a post-2020 America.

USA Today reports very pithily what New York Mayor, Rudy Giuliani, had to contend,

> 'What I did for New York City, Donald Trump will do for America', he said. Giuliani was part of a series of speakers that focused on the GOP's opening night theme of 'Make America Safe Again'. Giuliani, a former Republican presidential candidate in 2008, was chosen because he led New York City in the aftermath of the 9/11 terrorist attacks, coordinating emergency response and acting as a voice of reassurance'.

Going by what American historians have written, the global American objective, imbued with a messianic zeal, renders Washington capable of engendering 'Reassurance' and 'Regulation' amidst the American homeland and its doughty inhabitants. If the New York City Mayor does not run the risk of being bracketed with George Bush, Sr, then why do we intend to reserve our criticism for a flamboyant Donald Trump? USA has always been a nation striving at inclusion though antecedents remain in the coarse part of its territorial expansion. Still, we can ask a question to ourselves, 'which nations have not suffered from a strenuous and stultifying xenophobia'? The US though an archetype power hub is not much different as the long-drawn post-revolution trajectory of growth and integration was run by an undercurrent of larger-than-life personages who often contradicted with the American myth but ran true to the national interest during heady times.

Hillary has also been critiqued because of her usage of the government server for her electronic correspondence. This might not be an apt brick to hurl at her, but it is the new-world, entrepreneurial and unofficial elan of Donald trump that might be the perfect panegyric to go for. It might not amount to a personification of the grandiloquent American Dream, but the proximity to it is an infectious paradigm despite its rough and non-pedigreed edges. Obama has been attacked for signing up the nuclear deal with Iran despite its stealthy move towards a nuclear power status and the Syrian–ISIS quagmire too mars the current administration. The candidate who can deliver stoutly on these foreign policy themes will be the imaginative choice for the pedestal. As it turned out, he has delivered on Korea and his stringency on immigration remains as the preset. The much talked about reforms in criminal justice, police reforms, race biases, a shaky but now-improving economics might be the other deliverables sought after by the average American voter. Still, the candidate par excellence who can deliver largely on a 'Deliverance deal' for the American Dream will finally emerge as the popular favourite as no one can deny that populism before the hustling is what the spectacle of elections is all about with all the contexts.

With Donald Trump as the President, an Indian foreign policy thinker cannot help but ruminate over the impact of this Republican presidency on relations with New Delhi. The US has been often criticized for being interventionist in its foreign-policy decisions and activities internationally.This is especially true of the SouthAsian region, Afghanistan, the West Asia, the American role in Iraq after the ouster of Saddam Hussein and now the impending final battle against the dreaded, hydra-headed Islamic State. The Syrian conflict, too, simmers, while India battles cross-border terrorism, Pulwama being a recent example. In such a challenging scenario, President Trump comes with his approach of withdrawing America from conflict zones. Some observers of IR have commented that with the American drawdown in conflict zones such as the Af–Pak region, Syria and South China Sea, India will have a better strategic and diplomatic opportunity to be part of these regions as they strive for stability. India may have more strategic leverage to carve out its identity in the regional crisis situations. This is what our Trump has called far in NSS-2017. It's a special role for New Delhi.

Trump comes with the official belief that 'the other' and the 'alien' are a threat to the United States and the rest of the international system. This might initiate a new bias against New Delhi as Asian allies such as South Korea and Japan, are being asked to take care of their own funding support instead of relying on the protectionist umbrella provided by Washington till now. Going by this isolationist logic, Pakistan, being India's bête noire, may be asked to relinquish the status of 'frontline state'. India can hope that with the Trumpism of drawing down the American expanse in South Asia, India can emerge as the 'regulator state' and do the balancing act in South Asia. Still, tackling Beijing and its expansionism in South Asia and the seas, might be too much to ask for nations such as India. China may emerge as the regulator-arbiter nation in the Asiatic space. American disinterest in conflict situations and general bilateralism might not be a cushioning development for India and South Asia. Pakistan runs the risk of getting isolated in event of such an inward-looking United States. The US Administration has already curtailed the all 1.2 billion dollars of aid to Islamabad.

Candidate Trump wooed the Indian Diaspora too, with his advertisement, calling for 'Ab ki baar, Trump sarkaar', on the lines of the 2014 Modi campaign.

Trump understands India to be a great nation on the move, a fact which has been neglected by the global community for long. He attended a few events of the Hindu Diaspora and urged the Hindu community to elect him. Republican Presidents such as George Bush, Jr, have been known to support India.

The Civil Nuclear Cooperation Agreement signed between New Delhi and Washington in 2007, might have run into civil-liability norms, but the Republican standpoint has been positive towards India, with the Republicans being the conservative and the regulated voice of American politics. The zeal displayed by Trump to combat global terror modules, is a welcome development for New Delhi as India is involved in a battle against cross-border terrorism in Jammu and Kashmir and Punjab. A tie-up with the global community with Indian and American common interests can be a bright development for the global struggle against terrorism. Who can forget Dilip Singh, Kamla Harris and Julia Gabbard!!

However, Trump had also mimicked an Indian call centre worker in one of his early campaign speeches, but that is part of the byte that the election campaigns are all about. Outsourcing of trade and jobs has been a point of divergence between both the nations, which makes Trump a staunch protectionist in the context of employment-related relations with New Delhi.

China was running a trade surplus of $366 billion with the US and Pakistan, utilizing American aid to the tune of $30 billion since 2002, was playing foul with Washington. Now Trump, as part of his China and South Asia policy, intends to right the trade imbalances. A Trump onslaught has come as a trade war in 2018, at a wrong time for China as its credit-fuelled economy might come to a halt. With the dragnet of terrorism hanging on Islamabad, Trump might isolate Pakistan through aid and in tandem with his isolationist streak in foreign policy, might ask both the nations to solve the conflict bilaterally. Pulwama genocide justifies what White House chas done.

The India–US strategic dialogue would continue and the recent avalanche of agreements in the sphere of defence and military cooperation might become a permanent element of the bilateral relationship. This holds true for the larger context of what nature of impact and fallouts will the tenure of President Donald Trump portend for the larger international system. Farther down the line, the Trump take on Saudi Arabia and the larger policy vis-à-vis the Iran versus Saudi Arabia schism, too, can be zeroed in upon with insights into the Islamic schism between the Shias and the Sunnis in West Asia.

President Donald Trump tweeted on landing in Saudi Arabia, where-in, the Saudi state head was brought on an aircraft car to receive the US President. The tweet expressed, "I have reached Riyadh and I am looking forward to the afternoon and the evening that lies ahead."[4] The royal welcome accorded to Trump happens to be that of phalanx of red, white and blue contrails as the Air Force One, hovered over Riyadh and the terminology used by the Saudi leaders has been "Historic". It is only the murder of the Turkic journalist, Khashoggi in the Saudi Embassy in Turkey, that has mired the US–Saudi Arabian allyship in a quandary in 2018. The multistory image of the President was another mainstay of the larger paraphernalia which accompanies Trump's visit to Saudi Arabia. The entire rubric of the crusade against ISIS and fundamentalist terror happens to be a prime time concern of the American dream and the intent to prepare the homeland and protect it with repeated fusillades against the global spread of the terror group internationale.

The entire visit and the proclivities of the American empire are pitted against the rising overarch of Islamic terror, which has already expressed its slithering expanse and impactful malfeasance in the nations premised in the European continent apart from the "territorial avatar" of ISIS in the hotly contested terrain of West Asia. Since a few years, the US has been attempting to forge a consensual coalition, as an adjunct to the global, "War on Terror", which envisages the "Sunni NATO" nations such as Saudi Arabia which can go ahead with the annihilation of the Shia expanse in West Asia.

Also, the US made attempts to normalise bilateral relations with Iran, but, with the advent of Trump, that thought pattern in the policy reached a change. Washington's strivings are on to forge a bond with the NATO countries with twilight zone nations, such as, Turkey and the traditional allies such as Saudi Arabia. The efforts have always been on the anvil in order to cobble together an edifice and a coalition to counter the Shia group of nations. Thus, an international front to counter global Jihadi terror can be what the "Global-Peace-Doctor" ordered for the day.

The controversial earnestness with which the President has donned the mantle in the US is, part of the global strivings with the objective being the containment of global terror groups such as ISIS, Boko Haram, Al-Qaeda, et al. The allegation which can be labelled at Washington is that the strike potential, which has been unleashed over West Asia, has not been replicated with the Korean antagonist, who is a perennial nation state actor which is recalcitrant in its own myriad ways and posturing. The Committee on Foreign Relations too says, "Islam's schism, simmering for fourteen centuries, doesn't explain all the political, economic, and geostrategic factors involved in these conflicts, but, it has become one prism through which to understand the underlying tensions. Two countries that compete for the leadership of Islam, Sunni Saudi Arabia and Shia Iran, have used the sectarian divide to further their ambitions. How their rivalry is settled will likely shape the political balance between Sunnis and Shias and the future of the region, especially in Syria, Iraq, Lebanon, Bahrain, and Yemen."

There is a proxy battle which has always been fought with the jehadi terror mongers attempting a novae façade of unity to wage a war of attrition against Islamic terror. Historically, too, the succession matter over who had to be anointed as the head of the religion was formed which divided Islam into twin sects of Shias and Sunnis. It was Ali Ibn Talib, who formed the name around which the Shias collaborated and congealed as one part of the Islamic schism. The Sunnis remained as the followers of the group of Mohammad. It is this sectarian divide which has been the brimstone over which several West Asian conflicts have been spawned and the myriad nations from outside the religion and the region have been involved in the regional drama as it unfolded through the last few decades in the twilight zone of international polity. The treatment meted out to the non-Arab Muslims too became a schism in the region and the Arab and non-Arab regions on the whole.

An American web portal informs us that, "Iran's Islamic Revolution in 1979 gave Shia cleric Ayatollah Ruhollah Khomeini the opportunity to implement his vision for an Islamic government ruled by the "guardianship of the jurist" (velayat-e faqih), a controversial concept among Shia scholars that is opposed by Sunnis, who have historically differentiated between political leadership and religious scholarship. Thus, one of the all encompassing and all pervading divisions between Shias and Sunnis has been over the issue of the amalgamation of the "Political" and "Religious," which is what the entire regional fracas is all about to a certain extent. The NATO argument too informs us, "What is to be guarded against is the all pervading expanse and the rise of the state of Iran as a regional power." The recent lifting of sanctions against the nation state of NATO has also been an achievement of sorts for President Rouhani, who is a reformist and has romped home as the victor in the Iranian elections with a thumping victory percentage of 57 per cent. Arab Spring too brought out Iran into prominence as the various nations were at least symbolically democratised, especially in the nations with a Shia majority. Tehran has mobilised the entire Shia communities across the West Asian firmament in order to assist the Government forces in Assad's Syria.

Thus, apart from the American concern of toppling the applecart of the ISIS, the Shia Iran's regional influence too remains a cause to be militated against if stability and stolidity has to be reached in the West Asian region. This is the quintessential West Asian dilemma, which America faces in both the short and long term. President Donald Trump has become the first American President to visit a West Asian nation as one of his initial visits abroad after entering the heady portals of White House. Trump arrived in Saudi Arabia to rebuff the various attempts at policy making by President Obama when he struck a clearly discernible nuclear deal with Iran and attempted a wholehearted rapprochement between the "Sharia nation" and the "Satan Nation" as has been the nomenclature employed in the generally adversarial and obnoxious narrative between both the nations.

The *New York Times* reports, "The Saudis treated him like royalty, with red carpets, lavish meals and American flags flying everywhere. They repeatedly used the word 'historic' to describe his visit, gave him a medal, projected a multistory image of his face on the side of the palatial Ritz-Carlton hotel, where he was staying."[5] It's the spectacle which forms the nascent characteristic of US Foreign policy which hinges on larger-than-life antics with US recently "missiling" Syria under the rubric of strict reservations being expressed by Russia. The Saudi foreign Minister was informed that the Trump Administration aims at downing extremism and the export of extremism by Tehran. In summation, the American standpoint in the Houthi conflict in Yemen and the proclamation of an arms deal worth $110 billion with Riyadh happen to be the other frameworks which bring together the twin traditional allies against an Islamic state which breathes its last in the bad lands of Iraq and Syria.

Thus, in the context of the shifting sands of International Politics and Public Diplomacy, the American context has changed and transformed a great deal within the dimensions of a quaint but 'rebellious metamorphosis'. It also looks into how the nature of President Donald Trump's interventions will pan out for the international system, is to be delved inside with incisive detail and discursive analysis. Still, the left wing's grouse in the context of the Millionaire

President's dream run and his eventual seating in the White House poses questions for the rogue nations, the recalcitrant nation state actors and the anarchists. They are the cabal who tend to run certain segments of the gullible Fourth Estate and the academia in the name of adhering to the blind alley of 'critical thought, introspection and avowed criticality'.

In the context of the American withdrawal from the Climate change accord at Paris, some of the observers are also calling it as the great Climate Change denial. According to a research exercise, Donald Trump has tweeted Climate Change scepticism 115 times. A few of the tweets stand out. It runs like this in 2012, 'It's extremely Cold in NY and NJ—not good for Flood Victims. Where is Global Warming?' Thus, the stylistic and personalized negation of the globally accepted and bandied about concerns and phenomenon remains a quintessential hall mark of the Trumped up American Dream. That's vintage Trump for you! The flamboyant American President has always stressed the indigenousness of development and the Truslowian 'American Dream'. He does not care so much about the ideals of Neo-Wilsonianism and the 'American idea' as championed by the likes of Dean Acheson. In another 2012 tweet, the Donald Trump as a realtor contended, 'We can't destroy the competitiveness of our factories in order to prepare for nonexistent global warming. China is thrilled with us'. Thus, the Pittsburgh factor instils a policy incline that might be perceived as an anti-globalization and anti-regime tilt, that, more or less leaves the Climate Change regime in a strategic lurch and a limbo.

It's necessary to transform the way the commoners think about development, civilization and the environment. In one reading of the scenario, it can be contended that the climate change debate is about the disparagement brought out by the ides of non-industrial and developing nations. This argument might be serving the wrong side, as, the United States is also responsible for the pollution that ensues in the larger environmental vortex. Still, the assertion can be somewhere between the twin ideals of changing the domestic consumption and energy consumption patterns in the United States and accepting the moral responsibility to delve inside the rubric of Climate Change dysfunction in the 'Third World'.

Historically looking too, because of domestic developmental and economic concerns, the Americans have not been clear about the other agreements such as the Kyoto Protocol. The United States is a signatory to the Kyoto Protocol, but, has not ratified the much deliberated upon protocol, and Canada, too, moved away from the protocol despite its glittering role in other human security paradigms. America accounts for 36.1 per cent of the 1990 emission levels of Annex I nations. It was accepted that the United States would cut down its disturbing emissions by an average of 7 per cent below 1990 levels. One methodology for the US could have been to contain the polluting corporates. The Americans called it 'economically irresponsible' and thus paved the way for a separate American Climate Change policy paradigm. Still, positing the leadership role of the US in the climate change negotiations, the *Washington Post* contended that US ought to lead with confidence as GOP can rethink the entire Trump decision and look into some market-based solutions to reduce carbon dioxide emissions. Granted, protectionism is the order of the day for GOP, but how can a 'total screech of a separation' from the Paris Accord be tenable for America?

To Ruminate and Consummate a Narrative ...

Interventions, Incursions and the Oregon trail in the far-off lands have been used to the left-wing and anarchist criticism, as the liberal democratic order always serves as the staple fodder for the diatribes of the 'critical order' and the 'other'. The United States of America has historically been known to stay away from the 'Entangling Alliances' of continental Europe but anybody, per se any American President who seeks a 'running away and shying away' from global responsibilities, in line with certain domestic political currents, is bound to do injustice to the *larger Hyperpuissance, America: the Overarch and the great power mantle and halo of America, and the Fortress, America: the grandiloquent and shimmering citadel upon Mount Sinai.*

The defence and the championing of the legalities of the American interventions are a rare occurrence in the literature on the artifice of pre-emptive war. Still, the practice and the American striving to cobble together a defence of its interventions in far-off lands, is, a modus operandi that has been seldom dabbled in by any Asiatic, lesser than that by an Indian. It's an Indian affront to the academe that there is more than 'some water' left in the 'legalities' of American incursions in nations such as Spain, Louisiana, Vietnam, Afghanistan, Iraq and Syria. In a manner, in the contemporary context, the Americans are bound to be defensive but the same sovereignty poser can be labelled the way of the left liberals.

Critics, the world over, have stymied the cause célèbre of the grandiloquent American nation as the nation has allegedly infringed upon the autonomy, the sovereignty principles and realities of several receptacle nations. America is blamed with the allegation that its military interventions and "boots on grounds approach," have obliterated the indigenousness and the sovereignty of myriad receptacle nations, who, were forgetfully crisis ridden. Apart from this scale of reference, has any sane scholar ever ruminated and discussed the sovereign rights and manoeuvring space that has not been accorded to the mighty nation down the years. It's definitively a striving on the part of the author to delve inside the logic of the 'victimhood mentality' of the American nation. The United States of America, with its assiduously acquired might, is perched atop a perilous perch as the myriad nationalities in the third world are jealous of the American achievements with a capital, 'J'. Akin to the other smaller and micro nations, a bit of empathy and patience that must be had with the avid proponents of the 'American Dream', the American plight and unfortunate penchant of being lampooned and critiqued by all and sundry in the planetary space.

Thus, in a way, the American space has to reinvent itself about its defensive conditionality vis-à-vis the legal issues involved in the context of a pre-emptive war. Instead of being on the political and diplomatic backfoot, the American space can expand and distend akin to the halo of the batsman in the game of cricket as the batsman dances down the batting crease to lift the bowler out of the cricket park. The United States warrants a 'reinvention and a re-stressing' of its ethical and moral premise. It is this magic mantra that President Donald Trump has provided to his nation and its people who can clamour restively about the policy shenanigans of the American President, as, he dons the mantle of the quintessential need of the hour for America, that is, 'America First'.

Observers and practitioners of International Law might refer to the idiom of 'Just War', as, being the scapegoat for the American lawmakers, but, that is a fundamentally unflawed premise upon which nations, their people and establishments all across the Planet Earth have set their sovereign defences. The war to end all wars has to be fought and strategized upon within the rubric of International Law and International Relations with the attendant norm setting and US can do it better than all others. It's not exactly a battle-station geo-psychology, which we are talking about here, but a planning stratagem and preparation for securing a besieged homeland that the United States of America attempts to attain and achieve for itself.

Frankly, it will be a welcome exercise to look at the theme that how a defence of the American interventions pans out in the future, but the author strives to initiate a phase of that kind or a stage of that kind from a scholar personage stationed in India and emanating from the larger Asiatic space. Thus, in a manner, the author strives to assert that all is not well with the select ruminations of IHL, the interpretations of the Geneva protocols and the agreed upon/settled notions of international and non-international armed conflicts. Thus, in a way, the case law of the ICJ too can be studied through the diabolical eyes of the international lawyers in a manner that perennially aims to belittle the objectives of an America-sustaining vision.

The author strives to mount a balance in the favour of the United States of America. Going by the words of Alex de Tocqueville, the political firmament in America amounts to a balance in a twin-party system. The structure of the American political system is such that it is akin to a mortar mixing iron gong machine, that is, nowadays used in road construction in India. The machine takes in the mixture and comes out with a sludge that is good enough to the road construction material. In the same context, perceived through a biased eye of the IHL as deliberated upon in the book's narrative and through other law of conflict, the text mounts a mild defence of the charges and allegations on the United States as a free nation. This is the American and the author's dissent.

Firstly, the American establishment and the warring department militates against the age-old and insecure sinews of sovereignty, as proposed and cannily and avidly championed by the third-world nations and other crisis- and conflict-ridden nations and regions. Why cannot the urge of the American nation to predict its enemy manoeuvres and pre-empt them astutely be championed as another facet of the narrative on humanitarian interventions? It's the balancing-out of the anti-America rhetoric by some international lawyers that the narrative strives to emphasize as one of 'the most held' moral confrontations in the larger international system. Then, the splendid discovery is that the US and Trump need to manage the rise of China. Trump needs to learn to wear a veneer of predictability for the larger challenged brains of some of the IR observers and the larger academe. North Korea needs to be factored in, an assailable difficulty despite the recalcitrant nuke factor. Iran, too, under a new reformist President needs to be manoeuvred aside in the larger nuke and the regional equation. Also, Trump finally needs to wind up the war in Iraq against ISIS with the same intent being readily attempted in the context of the conflict in the besieged nation of Syria. The author strives for a sympathetic rendering of the American situation in its slew of humanitarian interventions along with the idiom of the Trump phenomenon being the new game changer in 'a spectacularly poised' Global polity. Can the sparkle of the red, blue and white contrails be comprehended by the larger comity of nations and other besieged and truly-free principalities?

NOTES

1. *The Hindu* News Report, 3 May 2017.
2. *The Indian Express* News Report, 3 May 2017.
3. George, Varghese K., 'I represent the People of Pittsburgh, not Paris', *The Hindu*, 3 May 2017.
4. *The New York Times* News Report, 28 April 2017.
5. *New York Times* News Report, April 28, 2017

Index